Brown

I Am My Father's Daughter

By Karen Denese Brown

Brown Girl Rich

A Wealthy Woman

I Believe It! I Receive It! I Walk in It!

Manufactured in the United States of America

10 9 8 7 6 5 4 3 2 1

Library of Congress Cataloging-in-Publication Data is available.

ISBN: 978-1-63769-872-3

E-ISBN: 978-1-63769-873-0

I Am My Father's Daughter

These precious moments of His Spirit Words

Belong

To

_____

Given By

_____

Your moments alone are precious and private;

spend them with God.

Dedication

Beautiful Sweet Lady of Purpose! You are called and set apart for great things. This book is dedicated to every woman who has heard the call of the Most High God and the ones who may not have heard the call or felt the unction to flow in your divine purpose. You are a beautiful treasure created by Jehovah God. You have been designed fearfully and wonderfully made. Every word in this book is for your heart, as well as to refresh your soul. Maybe you have gone through tough times, or maybe you have experienced the best times. Either path you have been on, I am here to show you that you can take the steps leading you to the greatest and most extraordinary victories. Take time to listen to the words of these pages as they speak to you. This is the call for you to be a powerful woman of God. I am glad to say that although you must push through the glass ceiling, you are now in another dimension that will require you to stay in His presence and listen to His voice.

Yes, feel His presence, hearing His words. Know in your heart that you and I are chosen to see the power of God work in us, and we are given the ability to go get someone else and bring them out. Alright, Girls! Let us go and get them!

Love,

Karen

Acknowledgments

I Am Wealthy with You

A very big special thanks to my heavenly Father, who has and continues to show me great and mighty things. He reveals secret truths and special mysteries because He is so *amazing*! In the times when I thought on my goodness, you said," Yes, my goodness!" Bless You, O Mighty God Jehovah! Nothing is impossible for you, and I enjoy seeing you do it. Great things! Yes, Great things!

I am thankful to my Mommie, who always continues to demonstrate and show me that honor, grace, truth, beauty, and most of all, the Holy Spirit is what we need to walk as strong, special godly women. Your love is the special invisible icing you put on every pound cake, and it is what keeps us sitting around the table, slicing it thick and thin to make sure it tastes the same all the way through. Yes indeed! ☺

To the Brown Boys and Brown Girls! Bill and Mergie's Children! You are the treasures that a girl needs to keep moving during it all. Lovehugs! Grouphugs! That's how we do it! Yes Indeed! We Glow! We Grow! We go get it! We must help to make it so! Your uniqueness as strong gems and jewels is price-less. I love you all! Whether the words are what I want to hear or not, they are the words that help me to continue to grow, flourish, and prosper in my walk.

To my pastor and friend, Apostle John L. Hickman, you always speak life to me and cover me with the Word of God, prayers, and support. I am blessed by your prayers, support, and love. Thank you, and I appreciate your leadership.

Love to all my spiritual family connections. I am thankful for your prayers and encouragement. Your hugs and love are so important to me. It is an awesome gift as we walk the faith journey.

Every person's part and word play an important role in creating a patchwork quilt for our purpose and destiny to take shape. It is who you are and what you have that connects to form this beautiful piece of art that is displayed for the world to see. Better yet, it depicts a strong and sweet revelation that it "does take everyone" to make it happen. Love you all very much.

Brown Girl Rich,

PK (Christgirl)

Table of Contents

Dear Daddy

(March 18, 2005)

I love you and thank God for you being the father He gave me. Thank you for showing me how to rely on God no matter what comes my way. Thank you for keeping me in a family where a momma and daddy stayed together throughout the vows that you shared. Thank you for showing up at school to pick me up when it was raining and picking me up from high school when the school was far away. Thank you for showing up at the graduation when I needed you the most. Thank you for celebrating my birthday. Thank you for allowing me to be your special daughter and sit on your lap to talk to you. Thank you for choosing me to teach Sunday school when I was a young girl. You saw something in me that no one else saw. Thank you for teaching me how to be the church secretary and tend to the church business. Thank you for showing me that serving God would be and is such an honor.

Thank you for giving me a nickname that only you could and would call me. Right now, I laugh to myself thinking of the name "Boss Hogg."

It was not about the weight but about the ability to command and lead, even though I was a little heavy and fluffy.

Thank you for protecting me from the big head boys who were only after one thing. Thank you for keeping me and anointing me every morning. Thank you for praying for me. Thank you for telling us to sing and putting us in the choir, usher board, the clean-up crew, the prayer team, and the women's mission board. You name it; you put us there. Oh yeah, even in the kitchen. Now, I understand the act and process of serving. Thank you for giving me the knowledge of Christ.

Thank you for showing me how to be independent and doing what needs to be done around the house. Thank you for not scolding me or whipping me when the truck was wrecked and a dent was left in it. Thank you for sending me to driver's education school and teaching me how to drive on the freeway. Thank you for baptizing me and being there in the water with me. All I could see was the mud between my toes and the minnows. The Lord only knows everything else that was in there. The mere fact that you were with me in the water gave me the boldness and courage to walk through it and get my baptism blessing. When you said you were with me, it kept me from being scared and fearful.

Wow, now as I think about it, according to God's Word, Isaiah 43 shows how God is with us and how He redeems us. Wow, He is with me. It does not and cannot hurt me because He is already going before me in the process.

Thank you for covering for me as I was growing up. Thank you for teaching me the Word of God. Thank you for being my daddy. Thank you for showing me how a man should take care of his family no matter what. Thank you for coming home every night. Thank you for being there when I went to school and being there when we were home in the evening. Thank you, Daddy, for keeping me as a baby because you could have been like those other men who did not keep their children. Thank you for your love and support when it was time to go to college. Thank you for wanting more for me. I love you, Daddy! Thank you!

Love,

Katie

P.S. Thank you for being my daddy in demonstrating to me how a man should love his wife as Christ loved the church and how I should expect my husband to do the same for me. Thank you for showing me how to serve my heavenly Father, the Almighty God, so diligently. You showed me how a woman should be treated by the man in her life as I watched you take care of Mommie in the most beautiful way. Thank you for being my "Daddy."

A Special Prayer

Heavenly Father, help us, your girls, to open and receive the manifold wisdom, your magnificent love, to experience it, and know it full well. Show us how to perceive Your greatness working in our lives as women who have been either with an earthly father or ones who have not known the love of a natural father. Thank you, Jehovah, for loving us with an everlasting love. You know us, and you have so greatly bestowed upon us one of the most prestigious titles and positions we can ever hold. We have the privilege of being "Our Father's Daughter."

So many women and girls have tried to find love in so many places. Heavenly Father, bring us into a place of love like no other. For that, Father, we say thank you. We appreciate you for breaking off the shell of fear and calling us forth out of the darkness into Your marvelous light to experience the beauty that was hidden for years. Now, we are embracing our potential, our gifts, our grace. Yes, we are now embracing our grace.

We are no longer looking back to see if fear would catch up. In fact, we can run forward faster with our confidence coat that you placed on us. We are beautiful women, blessed women, awesome and amazing wives, highly anointed women of God, wealth strategists, power-packing carriers of Your Word. You have equipped us mightily. For that heavenly Father, we say thank you. In Jesus the Christ name, amen.

We are "Our Father's Daughters."

Walking in our God-given authority.

I Am My Mother's Daughter!

Her love for me, in me, about me, around me! As I received the title of this book while I was in a secret place of worship, I always think of the beautiful, sweet treasures that our heavenly Father gives us. So, one of the sweetest gems and honors is my Mommie! I am laughing because I would not be my father's daughter if I did not have my Mommie. I am so thankful to have the ordained, beautiful, industrious, talented, Holy Spirit-filled, abundantly blessed, God's woman to be my Mommie. As I walk, talk, cook, work, minister, love, share, build, create, and just be who I am called to be, I am enriched by the grace and wisdom from my Mommie. My natural voluptuous grace and curves are directly from our lineage. Our smiles, our laughs, and our special touches and ability to do it all come from the sweetness that our heavenly Father poured in her and onto us. Her anointing to love us through some stuff is amazing.

We always laugh when she talks about old boyfriends and people who we have met and how when she gives us the note of saying, I am praying. So funny.

Women, we have so many great jewels and treasures that our heavenly Father blesses us with, and I am so astonished how He purposely placed us in our families and as I glean daily from her gift in cooking, making jellies, being a homemaker and worshipper, her love for telling us, "What God loves, and that is the truth," we are stronger and wiser.

I am thankful, and I am so glad that I am my Father's daughter because he made me a daughter of power, strength, wealth, wholeness, Brown Girl Rich fruitfulness, gifts, melodies, cakes, cookies, and all that sweet stuff that came straight from the throne room of God to my daddy to my Mommie! I am Brown Girl Rich! Hallelujah! On purpose! By purpose! In purpose! For purpose! Around purpose!

I bless you, Jehovah! In Jesus, the Christ name! Amen!

Introduction

I Know Who I Am!

When we step pass the veil, and we enter that place of grace that was originally designed for us in the beginning, we can see that our heavenly Father gets excited because He says, "She gets it now. She can experience all the wealth and beautiful experiences because they are her treasures I have for her. This treasure chest is no longer sitting on the bottom of the ocean floor. It has now been retrieved from the enemy's hands, and now she can open this treasure chest of jewels that are designed just for her." We are wealthy women because our heavenly Father has given us a beautiful name. He called us His own. Our faith kicks in the door that fear put up and tried to put a lock on it. Well, now that door has been opened, and it is just for us.

We can now proudly and boldly enter with the rightful inheritance that is ours. Hallelujah! The moment I felt that in my heart and spirit, I was able to declare, "I'm Brown Girl Rich!" "I Am my Father's daughter!" The "I Am who I Am" is my heavenly Father, and He lives within me. Wow! Wow! Just think, He said, "I have made you in my image. I call you by name. I know you inside and out." Yes, I have a natural daddy, but the beautiful part about it is that I came from my natural daddy, who came from my heavenly Father.

I am richly blessed in so many ways. For years, I was trying to attain something I already had. Yes, indeed, I stop chasing those things and people so that I could simply find me. *I am* who He says I am. *I am* my Father's apple of His eye. *I am* the anointed and appointed of the Jehovah God. *I can* do what He says I can do. *I can* boldly go and do what no one else has done. *I can* accomplish anything that I have the faith to do because He is working in me to do it by the power of the Holy Spirit. *I am* a creative person. *I have* gifts and ministries inside of me. My purpose and destiny are sure and blessed. Did you see that while reading what I just said? The more I say I am, the more I realize that the "*I am*" is working on the inside of me. Hallelujah! Read it again and say it with me.

The faith that we have only starts working when we accept that which was done on the cross by Jesus the Christ. Not by our own works, but by His works, the covenant, the connection, the extension of the Rod! That is why He said, "Stretch out your hand, Moses." Jehovah knew He would have a little girl who sat and watched her daddy preach the Word of God in this little country church. As I sat there, sitting near the window, looking down the winding road, with a paper fan in my hand, watching cars disappear as they drove down the road.

While all of that was taking place, the Word of God was saturating and filling me up deep within my soul and spirit. My eyes were watching, my ears were receiving, and my heart was filling up like a glass of pure water overflowing.

When it would be time, she would stand up, and embrace her grace, and walk the talk. Every time she tells the world about Jehovah's Word, it would cause her to draw close to Jehovah and declare Jesus is Lord and be filled with the Holy Spirit. That is why Moses had to bring the people through the Red Sea. The road was stretching from Moses to David to Jesus to us! Wow, we receive it, and we walk in it!

There would be a generation rising and not bowing their heads to the world but humbly submitting to the plan of the Lord God Jehovah. This girl is "Brown Girl Rich" She is "her Father's daughter."

She would grab the Bible, and the words would come off the page, become life to her, and cause her to step out of the old shell of fear, rejection, ridicule, abuse, ostracism, debt, lack, bad credit, bad men, hard relationships, scars, wounds of the past from friends, family, leaders, community environments, any other intimidating issue that thought it could block her walk. She decided that if God be for her, then who could be against her?

This time, there is no holding back, turning back, or giving up. This girl claims her inheritance back from the enemy and proudly displays her name as a daughter of the Highest God. His girl is you! His girl is me!

I Am my Father's daughter! Brown Girl Rich!

I am walking in my God-given authority!

The Lord God Jehovah knew what I needed. As a young girl, I would cry and tell my daddy while riding in the middle seat of the station wagon. My words to him, "Drive fast, Daddy." It was a small country town, and it was dark, but Jehovah would calmly have my daddy sweetly say, "It's okay, Daddy is driving." He would keep the car steady, and the sound of the engine would help me relax while waiting to get to the highway with the bright lights and populated areas. The city lights and noise gave me the indication that I was close to familiar ground. Funny, just hearing city sounds let me know that it was alright. He would say, "See, that was not hard." My daddy would tell us to watch as he drove on the roads, to watch the other cars and animals along the way. That is how our heavenly Father loves us and watches over us. We hear His voice, then we know, yes, it is okay. He would tell us to stay focused and not to worry about the dark because we had somewhere to go. That phrase alone is powerful.

Even as I write this now, I can hear our heavenly Father telling us, His daughters, not to worry about anything, stay focused, do not be afraid of the dark because He is driving, and we have somewhere to go. Hallelujah! My hands are up with praise, and my feet are running!

The peace of God was working then and showed this girl how to press past the stuff and the negative words that would try to hinder me and my steps. Jehovah God trained me how to keep moving amid it all.

You see, during the darkness, the treasure was formed and continued to manifest while it was not in the open. Let us talk about the metamorphosis of the butterfly. It is in the little cocoon, not with a light. It is quietly doing what it is supposed to do. It is creating its color; it is generating its perfectly designed flight pattern; it is strengthening its wings. So, here I am in my zone, creating words to fill my spirit and my heart. My purpose and destiny, my steps, my walk, my ministry, my DNA is lining up with the DNA of the Most High God! I am getting in direct formation with the plans, thoughts, and purposes of God's mind that He has for me. This girl knows that Jehovah has a planned purpose for me, and it is good according to Jeremiah 29:11.

As I stepped into faith, demolishing fear, and casting down doubt, what could be in my dreams and visions becomes a reality. I start to see the true living Word of God take shape and start forming into breakthroughs and victories that I could reach out and touch.

It is just like molding clay. I say it, I see it. I see it, I say it. The Word of God becomes a part of my life like never before.

My steps are sure, my faith is fixed, and there is nothing that can cloud that. If others come into the picture and agree, it would be nice, but if they do not agree, it is okay. According to Hebrews 11:1, faith is the substance of things hoped for and the evidence or proof of things not visible or seen. The substances are the tangible things that our Daddy has in store for us to receive, and my faith brings them into reality.

I stand on the evidence that Jesus did it for me. So, every time I stand and proclaim, I hear the Holy Spirit rising and saying to me, "Yes, Karen, this is what the Father's hope is good, and the future is greater than you can imagine."

As I see the power of Jehovah God start working, it becomes a crown of wisdom to my head; it becomes the signet ring of approval and the scepter of authority. The scepter of authority is that executive right given to us or bestowed on us as women with the set ability and grace to walk with the power to enforce or restrict. That is so awesome. We are a chosen, designed, equipped, and innovative vessel ready to do it. Not by my might, nor by power, but by His spirit.

The greater One is working in us to do His will and good pleasure by the words of Philippians 2:13 in His treasure chest for us. Esther had a metamorphosis experience where she stepped into the king's palace as a young girl from the community and was transformed into a woman who won the heart of the king.

"I Am My Father's Daughter" is a declaration for many women; in fact, every woman who feels like she did not have a lineage or one that she did not feel proud of sharing with the world. Either way, she can accomplish that big step to claim her God-given purpose and walk in it with Holy Ghost boldness. She can take the first step and say to herself, out loud not just within, but strongly, loudly, and very proudly, that she does belong.

She can say to herself, "I do have a purpose, I do have a destiny, I am a loved woman, I have supernatural extraordinary status, I am the King's daughter, I fear no one or nothing. He is with me always, He protects me, He called me, He chose me, He equipped me, He opened the way for me, and no one can change that!" Hallelujah!

She takes her rightful place of honor, prestige, and grace in the kingdom. She has a grace like no one else because she learned the wisdom of her natural father and observed the walk of her naturally beautiful mother, the queen.

"I Am My Father's Daughter" releases the woman from negative stereotypes and outlandish behaviors of the commoners who live by the world's standards. Every time God focuses on a woman, He takes her out of the pit and places her in the palace of His standards. She can now see herself as a valuable and priceless jewel. Everything a girl could want is found in her Father's kingdom. "I have everything I need." You, woman, who are reading this book, say that again with me. "He supplies everything I need." He knows our desires and wants, and He knows how to supply them to the full and overflowing. In Jesus the Christ name, amen.

When a girl speaks these words out in the open where everyone, including herself, can hear them, she can now see that in her heavenly Father, the King, she does have everything she needs. She can gracefully walk with her head up, and it will never hang down because she has received her royal status. She has now allowed our heavenly Father, her King, her Daddy, an opportunity to demonstrate His abundant love and fierce power for her.

He puts His stamp of approval on her and causes her to walk in confidence and an assured grace. She can do anything because she is her Father's daughter. There is no doubt about it.

Many women today have stayed for years in unfulfilled relationships and walked in unfulfilled lives because they were searching for love in all the wrong places. They sought for something they could not get until they came into the powerful realization that they were royalty. The power of a father's love, and not to mention the heavenly Father's love for the female gender, will break the yokes and chains that held women bound for years. Amen! I feel that because I know it to be true.

The process of a butterfly's metamorphosis represents the young girls who have been lost or locked into low self-esteem, self-criticism, or fear of self. Yes, there is a self-fear. This fear is afraid of being the woman God has ordained you to be. Not being able to accept the real person God has set her here on earth and created to be amongst all the other women.

The times when a woman has indulged in unhealthy relationships, actions, events, and any part of it, led her to a place where there was a void or something missing that needed to be restored. Today, in the name of Jesus the Christ of Nazareth, I declare that every woman who reads this book or has lifted their eyes to the One true living God is free today and released from the chains that held them captive.

When she stands up and walks in her God-given faith that comes from the heart of the Father that never leaves or forsakes her. As we read Hebrews 13:5, God made us a promise. He will not go back on His Word. We can take His Word and run with it. Jehovah declared the promise and covenant with us. You and I, along with every woman, can receive that strong promise and live. Live, I say, and not die.

Declare the works of the Lord. When you pick up your Sword, the written Word of God, Psalm 118:17, and Deuteronomy 31:6, He says it again. We have it in the Old Testament and the New Testament.

We have a fullness of that covenant. He has surrounded us

with an agreement with our heavenly Father that we will not have to walk in fear anymore or allow fear to be the bully it has been displaying. Fear has been demolished already. Jesus took it to the cross, and now we must believe it, declare it, and receive it. Most of all, walk like it. Change out of the old dreary clothes and put on your vibrant yet powerful royal gear.

Because Jehovah is holding us with His righteous right hand, according to Isaiah 41:10, we are women with a strong daddy who can lift us regardless of our weight. He comes in, lifts us up, and swings us around as we release a beautiful laughter, whether our hair is big afros, long and straight, fluffy or coiled, blonde or red. He not only just lifts us up to swing us around, but he is also lifting us up out of the sin that was so easy to be ensnared in from the old ties. He picks up his little girl and dusts her off from where she had fallen.

He is so cool with how he responds to her actions. He grabs her by the hand, lifts her up, hugs her, kisses her on the cheek, and says, "It's okay, Daddy's here." Do not you just love that! Oh, my goodness, it is so beautiful because He does not look at what happened; He draws us as his girls closer to make sure we know that we are loved. Thank you, Daddy, for loving me. We all have had those moments where you want to know if what you did was erased, and now you can walk with the clean slate to begin again. Sweet Jesus, our Big Brother, is right there to cover us, and the Holy Spirit is wrapping His loving arms around us to say He will take it from here now. As we surrender to the Holy Spirit, he will lead and guide us with all truth and keep us from going to these weird places where there are strange faces. He causes us to see the world at a different vantage point.

Our heavenly Father pulls us close to Him and squeezes us tight. He tells us that we are His daughter, and we can capture our inheritance and walk in the fruitfulness of His love. Another promise for us found in 1 Corinthians 2:9 lets us know that "Eye has not seen, nor ear heard." It begins to sink in and take root in our spirit by faith; there are things set just for us. When we say it out loud, our spirit man leaps up into the next dimension!

I think that deserves a shout right there! That means we are not average and what our Daddy has for us is not average either! We are walking in our supernatural extraordinary status! It is time that we stand up and take our ordained place, stop playing around, and change the page to get the new things that our Daddy promised us.

Wow, just think we have two types of eyes and two types of ears; that is a tremendous thing. We can hear and see what He is doing with our natural and spiritual senses. We have the double blessing. It is funny. More than what we could have imagined. Jehovah does some mighty things for His girls, and he is unveiling His girls to be mighty warriors for His kingdom. We are being unveiled and opened to experience the beautiful things that only Jehovah has saved for us.

It is like a treasure box or charm bracelet that a daddy gives his little girl. "I'm My Father's Daughter" is a treasure box for every woman, little girl, young woman, seasoned woman, or also for the men in the lives of every woman. It allows her to step into the big shoes that her daddy gave her, and now it is time they fit. Hallelujah! I know the plans that I have for you, plans of hope and future, as we put our eyes on the promise words in Jeremiah 29:11.

He already knows who will walk with you and how you will walk out your purposes and plans. It is now time to put on your powerful grace and love of Jehovah and time to throw off the old grave clothes and, most of all, shout! Hallelujah! I am shouting again. The darkness has been moved, and now the light has come! Arise! Shine! The glory of the Lord is upon us! Arise, Shine! What can I say, another promise found in Isaiah 60:1?

I am glowing because I am loved by my Father. "I am my Father's daughter." I am loved. When, I as a woman, connect with my husband, my children, my family, my work, my ministry. I am not just connecting with them because of relationship; I am connecting with them because of love.

Women, there are times when we have made choices, and we did things that were not pleasing. But Jehovah God snatched us from the enemy's hands. Glory to God! He said, "Oh no devil, that's my girl, my daughter, my seed. You can't have her." Hallelujah! Jesus, the Christ Savior, has come to save us and protect us. Now, we can walk around in our palace state. We are royalty; we have authority. This morning, when I woke up and felt the beautiful presence of Jehovah, I started to love Him, Jesus, and the Holy Spirit. I immediately heard this song about my authority rise in my spirit. I jumped out of bed and started jumping up and down, waving my banners to Jehovah! He said He gave us authority, I am a woman, I have authority, and I will use it in Jesus the Christ name! Amen!

If you are reading this book, you are called to get your inheritance and receive the victorious lifestyle. Maybe your last name is different; you can decide today to be rich in who you are and what you were made to be. It is only right to see yourself as our heavenly Father sees you.

Let us walk our walk in Him and let Him be the light they see! In Jesus, the Christ name! Amen.

In His love,

Christgirl

A Father's Daughter Affirmation

My wealth was given to me because "He knew me before I was born." It is a promise in my Father's Word. "Before I formed you in the womb I knew you [and approved of you as My chosen instrument], And before you were born, I consecrated you [to Myself as My own]; I have appointed you a prophet to the nations" (Jeremiah 1:5, AMP).

As we begin to love on our "heavenly Father," we receive a fresh release of His Spirit and His grace upon our lives. When we give Him worship and praise for who He is and how He continues to bring us to new levels of breakthrough and refreshing times for our hearts, He begins to fill us with the most opulent treasures straight from His heart to ours. Know it! Believe it! Receive It! Flow in It! In Jesus the Christ name, amen!

Prologue

Prom Night: How It All Started

Every time someone says these two words, "Prom Night," we immediately think of the pretty dresses on the young ladies and the cute tuxedos worn by handsome boys. These two words generally signify the time of young men and young ladies crossing over into their time of making decisions or evaluating choices. They are getting excited about going out on dates and dressing up, graduating, and driving just to the corner store. However, they are not cognizant of what prom night may open to them in the spiritual and natural realm.

This certain night was one of the most important nights of my life. I was dressed up and had partied with my friends at our Senior Prom. Well, as we were all leaving and laughing, discussing what we wanted to do next, one suggestion was shouted out. "Let's go to the beach!" It seemed like an awesome idea. So, I thought. I told my friends I needed to go home, change my clothes, and get some money from my mom. As I think about it, maybe I was subconsciously thinking they would save me from having to tell my friends that I really did not want to go. I walk into the house all dressed up in my formal dress, and with the intent of changing my clothes, my mom unlocked the door, and she looked at me with the "mama eyes." She politely asked me, "Kay, what are you about to do?" I said, "I came home to change my clothes, so I can go to the beach with my friends." She said, "I think you may want to ask your daddy." Funny, when you hear that phrase, you know it is about to change the whole scene. I immediately told her that he may be asleep, and I did not want to wake him because he worked nights and early morning shifts.

Well, wouldn't you know it, that night he was up already. He had changed shifts and was going in later. So, she said, "No, your daddy is up. Go in there and speak with him, and we will tell you what you will need to do." I immediately went to their room, and he said, "Hey Katie! You look pretty; how was prom?" I begin to share with him the *oohs* and the *aahs* of my Senior Prom night.

All the while, I was shaking and wondering how I was going to be grown at that moment and tell him, not ask, but tell him I was going to the beach with my friends, which included a male, whom I later realized I had a secret crush. Either way, you put it, Daddy was not going to hear it.

I began to share with him my plans to go out to the beach, which is why I was at the house. I was there to change my clothes. He sat very quietly, and then he looked at me. He begins to say these words, "You can change clothes, put on your pajamas and tell those friends of yours, they can go on to the beach."

I knew not to argue with him, because for one, he is my daddy, and two, he was bigger than me. So, I proceeded to the living room to speak with my friend (whom I had a secret crush on for years). He did not know it until years later. He said, "I can talk to your daddy if you want me to and let him know that I will look out for you." I gave him the look which indicated very emphatically, "You need to get out of this house now before you are told to go home." They left to go to the party and beach after prom. I went to my room and gladly put on my pj's for the evening and began to share with my sister the notes of prom night.

The next morning, I was awakened by mom handing the phone through the bunkbed opening. She said, "Kay, one of your friends said they want to talk to you; it's important." As I am listening to my friend talk on the phone, my eyes are getting bigger and bigger, all the while my mouth was opening wide. Wow, she begins to tell me all the happenings of the prom night beach party. All the things that I was telling my daddy were not going to happen most definitely happened. I am so grateful and thankful. My heavenly Father knew that my earthly father would protect me and use wisdom with how I was to be developed and loved. He told me about the things that were going on that I would not want to be a part of, and I should be about the things that were given for me to do.

When I think about all the events and happenings that the heavenly Father has protected me from, regardless of how much I cried to have or be in the midst of my steps for my purpose. But God! Somebody says, "But God knows everything, and he has a plan that is higher than anyone else." Everyone knows that when you are in the shadow of His wing, that he will keep you even as you are not keeping yourself.

Yes, this is so wonderfully true, He loves us very much and makes sure we are protected from the seen and unseen danger. Hallelujah! When I think about all the people who attended that party and how they became either pregnant, gave up their personal virginity, and compromised several aspects of their youth, it made me thank Jehovah God. I am not the perfect one, just the thankful one.

Thankful for Him saving me and keeping me. He shined the light and pulled me from the darkness to set me on a hill that I may shine as His prize possession. That is right, ladies; we are His prized possessions. His special daughters. We stand and take our rightful place in the kingdom with the dominion that he has given us. Now, ladies, arise! Now, ladies, sing! Now, ladies, we rule in the midst of our enemies. According to Psalm 110:1–2, He says to sit at his right hand until our enemies are our footstools. Then He gives us the scepter of approval with strength. Yes, I want what He has ordained for me. I am ruling and reigning in every area of my life with the Holy Ghost.

Let us take a minute and recall all the things that have been given up and claim them forward to our hands. Not just for us but everyone we know.

We, ladies, are the warriors our heavenly Father has trained and currently upgrading with our new ideas to make a difference and get our stuff. No holding back. David, in 1 Samuel 30, inquired of the Lord, and now we turn our ears to our heavenly Father to see what he is saying. Prom night is over, and it is the next morning. Light has come. The old has passed away.

It is a new season and a new you, and a new me. It is time

to pursue, overtake, and recover all. My worship will go before me as I turn to my heavenly Father!

Let our voices rise and make a sound that causes all of heaven to say, "The sleeping beauty has awakened. She has come out of her slumber and, now ready to do even greater things." Hallelujah!

More are for us than those against us. He says, "My little girl, Daddy is here, and I am with you. No fear. Just faith! Remember what I said before I formed you in your mother's womb." It will speak. In Jesus the Christ name, it will speak. Listen to the Spirit. He knows everything. He will guide you into all truth. It is so. Just listen and follow. Believe and receive. Watch and see. Grow. Blossom. Flourish. In Jesus, the Christ name. Amen. Love your heavenly Father.

He Touched Me

One night, I was sleeping. Well, let us just say I was in bed, but I was having the moments of tossing and turning a lot. I knew when I got in the bed; I was intending to sleep; however, Jehovah God had something else he wanted to say. I heard the Holy Spirit so clear instruct me to get my Bible and turn to this scripture. Song of Songs 2:10 (NIV), "My beloved spoke and said to me: Rise up, my love, my fair one. And come away."

Arise! My Daughter, *arise*!

Come with me, my daughter; I will not lead you wrong.

It is time for you to burst into a song.

Arise, my Daughter, I will shower you with My Love.

I will blanket you with peace like a dove.

Arise, my Daughter, your destiny is at hand.

You are now crossing into your promised land.

It's a New Season! Thank you, Daddy, for this New Season!

Sitting on Daddy's Feet

Yes, it was so sweet to get to a place where you know that He has it in control. You do not have to worry about the issues that were trying to grab you in places that were designed to be special. Here I am blessing my heavenly Father because you are telling me to get on your feet. I can go to places that I never thought I could go. I could do things that I could have never done. Here I am, Father, sitting on your feet. Here I am, Father, on the plan you have for me. I am your daughter, and I look to you for directions. I cannot do it on my own. I need you to take the steps, and as you take the steps, I am in the place where you want me to be.

As a little girl, we could not wait until our father would come home from work or just as he was walking around the house. There were some who would want to get the candy out of his pocket, and there were some who would want to get on his feet and walk where he walked. I was one of those little ones who would sit on his foot. As I sat on his foot, I would hold on to his leg and grab on tight, laughing and looking.

As he would walk, you could feel the strength and the love. He would just laugh and chuckle loud and strong.

He would say, "Hold on, Katie, Daddy going to the kitchen, or Daddy going to wash his hands." Wherever he went, I went,

I would not question what he was doing, and I would be in a safe place. He would sit at the dining room table; I would be sitting on his feet. I was at his feet. Wow, even as a little girl, I was more comfortable at his feet than at any other place. I would have to be someone near my father.

This was a place of comfort, truth, strength, purity, and love. I trusted his plan of what was in store or the direction he was taking me. It was his plan, not my plan. His feet always moved forward. As he moved forward, I, while sitting on his feet, would see the other stuff moving far from me. I would just laugh and giggle as I would press my cheek to his leg with my arms holding tight to him. It is such a beautiful and loving daddy's way of protecting his baby.

Daddy knew where he was going, and I was willing to go where he was going. Not sure as a little girl what it all meant. It was an experience.

It was a choice to get on his feet or run around the house playing. I wanted to cling to my daddy. I wanted to be near and receive what he had for me. After a while, he would say, "Okay, Katie, here you go." He would give me a quarter or a special treat that was not visible to everyone's eye. The candy might have been sticking out of his pocket, but he always had other treats deeper in his pockets that were not for the natural eye.

They were sweet treats like honey buns, cookies, dollars, gum, pens, or something different that he may have found. He was a special daddy. He would give good gifts to those who would hang around and look for more.

A daddy's desire to give special treats. As a little girl, I thought these gifts were the most special gifts. They were special to me and were just for me.

Now, as a young lady or woman, however, I may be perceived in other's eyes, I am still my Father's little girl. He has special gifts and treats deep down in his pockets. Deeper in the Spirit. These gifts are just for me, and I sit on His foot. I am clinging to His leg of strength, His truth, His love, His purity, His grace, His mercy. He is my Father in heaven, and I know He has a special connection to me. The place where we meet and where we converse is special and sweet.

He loves me, and I love Him. He knows the deepest things inside me, and the deeper I go in Him, the more they are revealed.

He is God, and I want what He has for me. I am now walking with His strength and abundance. I see Him and receive His Word in my life. The color of who He is shows so bright and brilliant. His majesty and power are what matters to me.

He is Jehovah God, and there is none like Him. Oh God, bless You for the directions and steps You are walking. I sit on Your feet. I go where You want to take me. There are places, naturally and spiritually, You are taking me. There are people I am to meet and connect with to accomplish the plan and purposes of our lives. They are out there, and they need Your Word. As You move forward, I move forward. The past is behind me, and the new is happening. The world needs You and Your touch. You may use me to touch the world with Your Word!

Designed and Certified for the Father's Kingdom

"The Father has the ability to change the name and destiny of a child. He can rearrange what was spoken over your life." Let Him.

My intimate time with the Father has increased my spirit tremendously. I have found out that no one can substitute His love and warm compassion for me to see Him in the realness of His presence. I yearn for the quiet times, candles burning, soft melodies playing in my spirit while we commune with one another. I love Him so much, and I now understand that my heavenly Father has a place in my heart that only He can fill.

At this time in my life, I see people searching for the things of this world, but He softly draws me closer to Him and causes my desire to become His desire. My heart wants to beat at the pulse of His heart. I want to get in the vein of His love and feel the constant flow of His liquid love. At times when I could not hear, He said to me, "My darling child, I never left. I was carrying you all the time. Keep looking to me." I had to release all the things that I wanted to experience to Him, so He could truly bless me the way He would.

My heart and ears are opened to God for Him to come

in and take out what does not belong. I want to love everyone and see where He is taking me. I am truly walking by faith. He is using the Word to truly deliver me into areas where I never thought I would be. He is using His love to deliver me from those things that tried to hold me that were not of Him.

He has manifested Himself to me through song and poetry. My heart rejoices to see and encompass His never-ending and always abounding love. He rejoices over me with special melodies, and He is giving me a new song and joy in my spirit. There is an igniting in me of a renewed passion to thirst and hunger after His righteousness.

I wanted to clearly hear God's voice for myself. I now seek for the truth and the promise of His faithfulness. Oh, how if I could take what I have found out and what I have experienced to show to those who will listen and receive. Our heavenly Father is not concerned just about things, but He is concerned about the natural and special intimate times we should be worshipping Him. It is about praising Him for who He is and not for what He is doing or giving us. What can I give to my heavenly Father that will demonstrate how much I love and adore Him? It's a yielding heart full of love and worship for Him. It's an offering of simple trust and belief in Him and knowing that He has already provided all things in all-sufficiency. Whew! Talk about being in love. True love.

I can dedicate my life as a woman of God to please Him. I please Him by showing others who He is and how they can live a life wholeheartedly devoted to Him by walking according to the Word of God that will touch our families, our spouses, our children, our churches, our jobs, our communities, and those whom we encounter every day of our lives. How we are with God will either turn them to Him or force them away. Which one is your goal?

Take this time to get with the Father, give Him intimate time, and see how He will be there. Experience a love so divine that is like no other. Much love to you, and enjoy a liquid love poured out upon you!

BGR _____

_____

_____

_____

_____

_____

_____

_____

_____

_____

_____

_____

_____

_____

_____

_____

_____

_____

_____

_____

_____

_____

_____

_____

_____

_____

The Prophecy,
Our Life, His Daughter

"And afterward I will pour out My Spirit upon all flesh; and your sons and your daughters shall prophesy, your old men shall dream dreams, your young men shall see visions. Even upon the menservants and upon the maidservants in those days will I pour out my Spirit" (Joel 2:28–29, AMP).

Now write your faith confession with this scripture:

_____

_____

_____

_____

_____

_____

_____

_____

_____

_____

_____

_____

_____

_____

_____

_____

_____

_____
_____
_____
_____
_____
_____
_____
_____
_____
_____
_____
_____
_____
_____
_____
_____
_____
_____
_____
_____

Purpose, Love, Truth, Destiny, Power, Authority, Favor, Wisdom, Abundance, Promise.

Arise, My Daughter!

"My darling, it is time for you to rise.

I am doing wonders before your eyes.

I want to show you a whole new world.

You are transforming into a beautiful lady from a girl.

Love in Me is yours for the taking.

Seek Me and see what I am making.

Your time to come forward is now.

Keep trusting Me to show you how.

Arise, my daughter. It is time for you to come.

What you are looking for is already done.

Take hold of the promises that are yours.

I have the key to open the right doors.

The power you possess is strong.

Who you are will be revealed; it won't be long.

You are so beautiful in so many ways.

I knew you before you were born.

Put on your robe of praise and blow your horn.

It is time to praise, give thanks, and live.

I have given you a heart to give.

Arise my daughter—I want to deliver you.

I want to bring you out and see you through.

Break forth like the dawn; you are mine; I call you my own."

Independence—A Declaration of Freedom

July 8, 2010, 10:30 p.m.

I changed my mind—I do not follow what I used to be; I am what I am called to be!

A new mindset! A stronger desire!—Wow, God, thank you for this Holy Ghost fire!

Declaring a new thing—pulling down the old, pushing forward—letting go of the ties. Who would have thought? I am glad I can expel the lies.

Thanking you for cleaning up the drama and the mess,

I receive more and nothing less!

Breaking and pulling down the stronghold that thought it could be a family friend. Well, I must tell poverty, lack, fear, procrastination; they are stopped. This is now; that was then. Breakthrough is here, and it is mine to call forth! There are many dreams that I must birth. The visions and the desires all have a place! It is time to wipe the tears from my face! Wow, a new me and a stronger girl.

My heavenly Father has come to bless my world. For so

long, I hid and left the issue to be dissolved by the Holy Spirit. Today, I declare that those things are broken off me and my family. We are healed, set free, and delivered.

Thank you for opening the door for me so that I can. The world to tell about Jesus, I can go forth and reach.

Wow!

I Am My Father's Daughter!

A Woman of Identity

The ability to know who you are.

I am my Father's daughter.

What is in Him is in me.

I have His DNA.

He speaks—I speak.

He sees—I see.

He creates—I create.

He arranges—I arrange.

The atmosphere changes when He enters the room.

The atmosphere changes when I enter the room.

I am a woman of identity.

I know who I am.

I am fearfully and wonderfully made in Him, and I know this full well!

Receive daughter! We are made in His image, and we are beautiful.

A Love Song of a Daughter

I am my Father's daughter; yes, I am.

I speak what thus says the Lord; I have His DNA; I have His character; I have His love; I have His eyes; I have His lips; I have His hands; I have His feet; I have His ears.

He is on the inside of me. I am fearfully and wonderfully made. No one can tell me anything different. No one can touch me like Jesus! He is real. He called me and chose me to take a stand. I serve one true God. He holds the key to my destiny. He knows what He put inside of me. He made me to be strong. When He works, it does not take long. You created me to praise and worship with my heart. He knew what I would be from the start.

Yes, I am my Father's daughter. He formed me when He put the world in order.

He fashioned me by designed as His daughter.

Oh yes, I am blessed and full of beautiful things. He gave me a voice to sing. Transforming and conforming to the plan of the Father.

I move forward! I move forward! I move forward.

Yes, forward!

An Esther Moment

The King Will Do What He Is Supposed to Do

As a woman of excellence, we must develop a plan. We cannot just run out and expect things to happen without bursting out on the scene. A plan must be in place. God will do the rest.

Sometimes, you must make a move. It does not matter what people think. When you step out on faith, it is not going to feel comfortable. It is an opportunity for God to do what He said He will do. Hold on to Him. When you make the faith jump, it will move you closer in your walk with God.

Esther had the favor of God in her life. She can go to the King and get what she wants. Here enemies are trying to take her out, *but God* gives her a plan on how to turn the enemy's traps he set for her back on himself. The Lord holds the King's heart in His hands. He turns it in whichever way He wants. When you need a decision to be made on your behalf, and the King can give the decision, trust God.

The Father will cause His heart to be turned and purposed to do what God needs Him to do, to make it right, regarding the promises made. Amen. The King will not be able to sleep until He has done what He is supposed to do.

"Father Here's My Heart"

(A Prayer)

Heavenly Father, thank you for who You are with us. Thank you for touching us with Your healing hand—for You are Jehovah Rophe! Healer! You are the Lord God that healeth thee. You are our Jehovah God, who reigns supreme in all things. You are sovereign above all. Your majesty and power are not able to be compared! You have outstretched hands, and Your name is above all names. You are Hashem! What a mighty God we serve! You are our Shepherd. Thank you for guiding us. As we come before You, oh God! We seek Your face.

We come thanking you for a great revelation of Your Word. A great manifestation of Your glory. Oh Jehovah God, our Adonai, your Presence matters to us! May You be here as we pray! Let our words, songs, and meditations rise as a sweet fragrance, a precious aroma, and unique sound to Thee, Oh God. Thank you for creating us, Elohim.

Thank you for uniquely crafting us to be different, a royal priesthood, a holy nation, a truly peculiar people. There is none like You, oh great, Jehovah! You are I am that I am. What a great God You are. I praise you for You are El Shaddai. You are the many-breasted One!

You are more than enough. You do not run out. We do not run out! We are walking in the overflow. We are supplied with abundance! Our vats and barns are filled, and we can give to others out of our overflow! What a mighty God we serve! You have called us to a new place in You! A higher understanding and deeper revelation of Your love! Thank You for a beautiful gift! You sent us your darling son, Jesus, to be a sacrifice that we may live. He rose that we are walking in the abundant life. A blessed, rich, satisfying life that can minister to others in ways we are still discovering more of You! Oh, El Elyon—how high and mighty You are!

Oh, beautiful! Holy One! What beauty is Your name! A true Father You are to us! You are Abba, you are called Holy One as we lift our voices, and we cry out to thee, oh God! You are our focus! You are our sight! You are our truth! There is no deception in You. As we come before your throne this day! We submit what we thought we wanted to say. We just pray to You here is our heart.

As we come, we submit what we thought we wanted to go and do. We submit to Your perfect will. We submit to your plan and purpose for our lives. As You said in Jeremiah 29:11, You know the plans You have for us. Thoughts of peace and not of evil; to give us hope and a future. You said in your Word, Isaiah 55:8, Your thoughts are not our thoughts.

We have thought one way before, but You, oh God knows all. You are omniscient! You perceive all and have set it before we speak out of our mouths. Thank you for Your sovereignty.

Oh God, thank you as we submit—we yield, we surrender. We give ourselves to the authority of the Holy Spirit. You said in John 14:25 that He will teach us all things. So, today, Father, we choose to listen and be taught by the Holy Spirit! His plan is perfect because it is the plan You have for us.

For us to get the plan and the thoughts, oh Lord God, our Redeemer, our Master, we listen! We make it a point today to listen and hear what concerns You and what is in Your heart! We want to know how to war! We want to know the strategies and the new steps for the plan. We want Your prophetic release in our lives. We want to be in a closer relationship and fellowship with You! Our hearts are knitted to seek after You fully and totally. Oh Jehovah Nissi, You are our banner. Your banner over us is love!

Thank you for teaching us how to walk in unconditional love, which is a weapon that is not carnal but mighty through You. Love covers a multitude of sins.

Love protects, heals, covers, restores, and love is not concerned about faults. Thank you for Your beautiful love. Love is patient; love is kind. The truth of this love will bring others to Christ. Teach us to love, teach us to relate. Thank you, Father! You are Holy! We reverence You!

Our Father, which art in heaven, hallowed be thy name, thy kingdom come, thy will be done, on Earth, as it is in heaven! Give us (your children, your sons, your daughters) this day, our daily bread. Forgive us our debts, as we forgive our debtors. Those who have hurt us! Do not lead us into temptations but deliver us from the evil one. For Yours is the kingdom, and the power, and the glory forever. Amen! Oh, Father, we thank you as we come, and we are looking to hear more of You. We ask the Holy Spirit, the revelator of truth, knowledge, and wisdom, to come!

Show us what the Father will have us to see! Anoint our eyes with oil! Unveil our eyes, let us see; unveil our hearts, let us come to know. Thank you, Comforter! You soothe in times of hurt and pain. Come, Comforter, overshadow us like never with Your touch! Provide us with the confidence instead of fear; provide us with a truth instead of a lie. Thank you for giving us a new capacity to be filled up on the inside with Your power. A power that cannot be denied or described. A power that is magnificent, sure, more than we can imagine or hope according to Ephesians 3:20. Do it more abundantly! Hallelujah to Your name! Let Your healing and anointing flow through the secret places of our lives. Flow through the hospitals, the streets of communities, homes, workplaces, marketplaces, nations, corporations, governments, cities, states. Flow Holy Ghost with the Rhema Word of our heavenly Father. We, His daughters, take our place and declare the decree!

Atmosphere, be filled with the presence of the Holy Spirit! It has a new way of flowing; healing takes place! Anointing rests upon us! We are in the flow of the Holy Spirit!

We do not operate or move as the world does. Greater is He that is in us than he that is in the world! As we are here, Lord Jesus to worship You, to offer up praise and prayers. We also say we are here to listen, to be still, and know that you are God, as Psalm 46:10 tells us. You are the one whose voice is powerful. Your voice makes things happen! Your voice over the waters! Your voice is powerful and is full of majesty and as it tells us in Psalm 29. Your voice breaks the cedar. Yes, your voice, Lord, is what we desire this day. You said when we delight in You, You will give us the desires of our heart! So, Father, Abba, we come to love on You and make You are a delight.

You are what we want. Satisfy our souls, for we need You! Saturate us with Your love, presence, and power. You are God; You are almighty, You are beautiful, You are splendor, You are power. What a wonderful mighty God we serve. Thank you, Father, for giving us the ability to break through the barrier. You are the God of the breakthrough. So, today we call You Jehovah Baal Perazim! Thank you! As we run with You, we leap over walls and run through troops. The enemy plans have already been defeated, and we are delivered to help deliver others by Your grace. Hallelujah to the Highest God. Thank you for Your Shekinah glory filling our secret places! Fill us with Your power. Come Holy Spirit move in the air over our lives. We honor You! Be our Guide and Friend.

Thank you for communicating with us! We love to hear what You want to tell us! For we know that it is good for us. Tell us what is on the Father's heart regarding the nation, the communities, the children, the families, the financial realm, and marriages. Here we are. Open heaven revelation come, spirit of truth come, spirit of wisdom come, we are waiting on You to show us! Reveal to us! Enlighten us with the truth as Ephesians 1:15–18 says. You are El Roi, the God who sees. So, Father, we trust You.

We see as You call us to see. Thank you, Lord, for teaching us and instructing us on the way to go. We love you! Teach us how to stand still and see the salvation of the Lord as You told the Israelites in Exodus 14:13–14. As we stand still, the enemy that tried to come is rebuked, and we do not have to worry about it!

You said You would handle it. Thank you, oh God! We praise You! We exalt You. We magnify Your name! We make You higher than the situation, the issues, and the concerns. You can do just what You said You would do. As You said in Isaiah 55, Your word will not return to You void, but it shall accomplish what it was sent out to do! Thank you, Jehovah Tsidkenu, for You are the Lord God, our righteousness.

Thank you that You show us how to receive Your righteousness and be righteous. Thank you as we listen. Thank you as we take the time to hear what You want to say. You say great and mighty things. You came to Mary in a moment to share a great and mighty assignment. Oh Father, in her submission, she received a great gift and assignment. When she said, "Be it done unto me," she went through a transformation. Her life was changed; she was able to become more than what she was before. Her anointing became strong, and it was illuminated.

So, Father, we submit and say yes, we love you and will do the assignments! She was increased and endowed with a special touch and connection because of her favor and relationship with You. So, Father, we say, we receive what You have for us. We thank you! Tell us and share with us great unknown mysteries, mighty treasures, secrets, and beautiful visions! We receive what You have ordained and called us to be this day. We have an ear to hear! May our prayers during the night watches be an opportunity to declare, decree, set in place, and listen to the communications from Your heart to our heart.

You speak to us. Oh, God! We are here for You. Mary said, "Okay, here I am. What do You want me to do? I will do it!" Lord God, Adonai, Lord, our Master. We pray for the sick, the shut-in, the world meetings, the hurt and abused! The outcasts!

Oh God, reveal to us the one who is crying out in the shadows by themselves in the mornings, the runaways, the trafficking of young girls. Oh God, we cry out for deliverance and healing. Thank you for the ability to plant the seed. Thank you for the authority to pluck up, uproot, pull down, and tear down the enemy's plan and schemes. You are Jehovah Gabbor, God of war! Thank you for the full armor of You as we are clothed this day. Thank you, the Blood of Jesus is applied on every doorpost, and we are covered by Your hand. We love You! Pour out the assignments and the places on the map we are to pray and intercede for daily.

Navigate our prayers to the corners and the homes. Let us pray to see the salvation of the Lord come forth. Thank you, Lord. Teach and instruct us the way we should go. Holy Spirit be our compass! Be our light! Shine in the areas of darkness! God be glorified in the earth and in our lives. Oh, Holy One, we love You so much! We adore You! Ministering and guardian angels go and encamp around those who are needing a special touch. Bring gifts of peace, love, and serenity.

Thank you, Father, for You said where two or three are gathered, You would be in the midst. We thank you for being here! You said, "One can chase a thousand, but two can chase ten thousand." So, Lord, thank you that many are saved and delivered because we come to pray and stand in the gap. Thank you for truth, consecration, sanctification, and the spiritual disciplines being exercised in our lives.

Holy Spirit, thank you for communing with us this day. Thank you for Your special anointing for the broken marriages, the lost children, and the persons who are in debt. Anoint the sick, bring healing: emotionally, mentally, physically, and spiritually. Oh, Father, You are high and lifted up. We cannot do it without You! Thank you for flowing Your healing virtue through the lives of Your people! Your healing light comes in Jesus' name! Hallelujah! Oh, praise you for You are God!—I *Am* that I *AM*—God of Abraham, Isaac, and Jacob. Thank you for being the One true living God who we shall have no other gods before You. Thank you, Holy Spirit. Minister deliverance and healing. Heal from the inside out! Thank you for Your grace and mercy. Hallelujah! Lord!

As we have come, we ask you, Lord, that Your healing flows in the lives of those that are praying daily. You know every name, need, and desire! Thank you, Lord, for Your omnipotent power! We thank you in advance for what You have already done in the spirit. We love You. In the name of Jesus, we believe the prayers to be answered. As You have told us in Matthew 11:28–29. That as we pray, we believe it according to our faith. It is done. Hallelujah! In Jesus' name, amen! Thank you for Your favor and wisdom. Thank you for the anointing upon our lives. Thank you for multiplying peace, healing, and blessings to us! Thank you for the refreshing and refilling of your children. Thank you that we walk victoriously because You tell us in Isaiah 41:10. That You will uphold us with Your victorious right hand. Strength multiplied because we wait upon You, and You renew the strength. We soar high on wings as eagles. We run and not grow weary. We walk and not faint. Hallelujah!

Thank you, Lord, for who You are! We bless you, Jehovah! Thank you for Your presence with us. Thank you for our countenance radiates joy, and we are Holy Spirit-filled. We can go and be a blessing to others! We love You, and we are Yours. You be our God!

Father, I am just saying, I love You! We love You in Jesus the Christ name, amen.

"The Girls Are Right… Says Jehovah God"

(Numbers 27:1–11, NKJV)

How many times have you heard that phrase? I was amazed when I first read this story in the Bible. It is such a privilege to walk as Jehovah's daughter. He loves us so much, and He never leaves us or forsakes us. His powerful touch rebukes the enemy's plans. He holds us in the palm of His hand. When there is no one out there speaking up for us, Jehovah God says He has the say-so over what we have and how our purpose was formed and shaped. He made us in His image. He knows everything about us and where our land is located.

In this story, these girls' father had died in the wilderness, and they were not among the Lord's people, or you can say they were not part of the "in-crowd." They were out there on their own with brothers. However, when it was time for the portions of the inheritances to be distributed, the people were going to overlook them. Can you say, but God! Hallelujah! These girls had a boldness to ask for what they wanted. They went right up to Moses and the leaders. The beautiful thing about it all is they went by the doorway of the tabernacle of meeting. Glory to Jehovah God, the place of worship. The place where they met with Jehovah was the very place they went to request their inheritance.

As they were entering the doorway of the tabernacle, they were embarking on a new journey out of the old into the new. Their purposes and destinies were about to be changed. They were about to be shifted up and out of the obscurity of their past. All the hurt and pain they had experienced were immediately erased, and they were receiving a clean slate for the kingdom. It was time to advance to the new place. Time to pack their bags and go north. A new season and a new joy. Pulling off the fear and putting on faith. Wow, these girls were given a new lease on their walk. Old things had passed away, and behold the new thing! Hallelujah! They opened their mouth and changed the plan. What! Yes, they did not just sit there and wait; they went in and approached the very one who was holding their stuff.

Anytime there is a door present, it presents an opportunity to cross over into a new dimension or somewhere different than before. A new realm of His love and grace bestowed on us His daughters. No more fear. Think about it, these girls broke barriers, glass ceilings, restraints, and crossed areas that were usually set for men. It was about a different type of women's liberties or women's rights; it was about getting what was rightfully theirs.

You and I have a right to what our covenant consists of with our heavenly Father. So many times, because we have experienced some type of pain or rejection, we had not approached the desk and requested what is rightfully ours.

"The Girls Are Right…Says Jehovah God"

Recently, I had the opportunity to sit and listen to several powerful professional women. The common thread as they laid out the fabric women in the workplace was such as that we as ladies must not only walk up to the table but expect the space to be made for us to take a seat at the table. We are also to open our mouths and use our voices for good. Whatever the cause is, whether it is for someone else or most of all yourself. We must get out of the shy zone and get into the fly zone. We are eagles too. Our heavenly Father has made provisions for us, and it is our time to stand up, step up, speak up.

He knows exactly what we need when we need it. We have the Holy Spirit to help us understand and flow with the wisdom to see beyond the smokescreen of the enemy. Our eyes are anointed to see clearly, and our ears are tuned into the voice of our heavenly Father. He will not lead us wrong. He will always have the clear path to those treasures stored up, and He knows exactly when to release them as we stand in faith. I am thinking to myself how they must have felt walking into the place where there were only men and maybe a few other women who were in the midst. All eyes on them looking over their turbans and garments. Questions, gossip, rumors, and unkind words being spoken of them. Wow, an atmosphere full of heavy thoughts, but there arose in them a strength that would push past the biggest, the baddest, the oldest, the youngest, or even the most important because what is mine is mine. I am coming to get it. Once, heavenly Father said, "The girls are right!" I would have taken off running, shouting, turning flips, and most of all praising my Daddy! Because He heard my cry and saw my tears. He knew my fears and understood it all. We are the girls that changed the laws! That is how I am feeling right now.

After they received their inheritance, the laws and regulations were changed to help others. Think about it. What do you and I need to open our mouths to say to change a law, release an inheritance or just get our stuff? Yes, sisters, it is time to change the rules, be the gamechanger, and most all set the captives free! Hallelujah! Breaking barriers and trailblazing is what I do. It is who I am! Created in my Daddy's image! There is a sound in us that cannot be quiet! Shout with me! Now! Hallelujah to the King of kings! We are ready to take the land! Because He said so! In Jesus, the Christ name! Amen!

I Am Working with My Daddy

(Nehemiah 3:12, NKJV)

Our heavenly Father is so amazing, and He has equipped us with so many gifts to accomplish the most outlandish assignments. I remember when I was learning to ride a bike, and my daddy was right there. He was holding my hand to make sure I had the confidence, and I had the complete assurance knowing that he was right there the whole time. Of course, there were times when my bike would do its own thing, and I was finding the ground as a cushion. It is funny how things work because our heavenly Father will be right there to pick us up.

So, as I am thinking about the times we were working with my daddy, it causes me to be so thankful for learning how to build. There were times when my daddy was working in the yard or working on the church to get it ready for worship, and he would have us right there. I am reminded of the scripture in Nehemiah 3:12. All the families were assembled at their designated posts to help rebuild the wall. I was reading this passage of scripture, and it just blessed me so much. While all the families are building and how the Nehemiah was describing all their duties and who were the leaders of each tribe or group. Then, a special phrase pops out of all the words written. These words just leaped out of the page and created this big bright light shining so strong in the atmosphere. It boldly said, "And next to him was Shallum the son of Hallohesh, leader of half the district of Jerusalem; he and his daughters made repairs." Oh, that spoke volumes to me! I was so excited to know that Jehovah God, our heavenly Father thought it to be so important for us to know that He will use us to rebuild the wall, and He will be right there with us. Yes! We are well able to conquer the land and do it well. No fear and no holding back.

We can run to the battle with our weapons and win! So powerful! I am my Father's daughter, and I can walk in my God-given authority. Just think, whoever these girls are, they are not aware they are making history, and they are in the most famous Book in the world. Their names are not mentioned; however, they are doing a great assignment. How many times have we looked to make sure our name was written, or some-one gave us credit for a job done? This is so profound. If we just do what we are supposed to do, we will get our just reward of notoriety and breakthrough at the same time. These girls were a part of a major move of rebuilding a nation with the construction of the wall.

Every time we go to our knees in prayer or call on our heavenly Father on behalf of someone, we are rebuilding the wall. Prayer is a powerful assignment and gift that we have been given. It is up to us to open the gift of prayer and let it be used for His glory. We make a quality choice to make up in our minds, and we are being determined to win. It is His pleasure to do His goodwill. The moment we start looking at the task as a big thing, then it becomes a hard thing. But, when we say I am working with my Daddy, it gives a whole new meaning about what we are called to do.

Wow, when I am at home and maybe feel alone, I can call on Him, and He shows up to comfort me. My Daddy gently hugs me and says, "It's all good." "You're my girl; I will bless you." At that very time, I grab my joy paper (my tissues) and wipe my eyes and say thank you to Him for my heavenly Father. He knows exactly what to say and how to say it. Working with my Daddy is a powerful statement because when we think about how and what we do daily or whatever it is we do, it brings a big question to mind. *Who do you do it with?*

A few days ago, I was sitting and thinking about a few projects, then all sudden, I heard the Holy Ghost speak so clearly. He said, "Make sure you do it with Me." "With Me, all things are possible; you can do all things, you can run through troops, leap over walls, operate in a new dimension, and breakthrough portals. You can create, be innovative, and be prolific.

You can be quiet or loud, overjoyed, refreshed, and function in positions like no one else can." "The main point is that it has to be with me." My relationships and communications must be with Him. When we are moving forward in the steps to accomplish all these purposes and destinies, we must pull away from the world's standards and ways, with the strong intent to work with our Daddy. This is so profound because every time you hear of someone working on a roof, fixing plumbing, and building walls, you would automatically think it was a man who did it. Today, things have changed somewhat. Because the man is somewhere in other capacities or maybe just not present in the home, the woman must take on roles that may not ordinarily be what she would do. However, she has the boldness, the courage, the know-how, and the anointing to do it. I am reminded of a time when I needed my plumbing fixed, and this gentleman came to do the repairs. So, I see this big pickup truck pulling up and beginning to back up with supplies, ladders, and every plumbing fixture you can imagine. As the person begins to get out of the truck, I see ponytails and pink tennis. Wow, funny, it was a lady. The man said, meet my daughter. Yes, his daughter was the one driving the big truck, then she went to get the ladder. She grabbed the ladder and laid it against the house. She began to scale the ladder without any hesitation. She hopped on the roof and began to assist her daddy. Yes, I was so blessed to hear and see this father-daughter team moving in sync, completing the task or assignment if you will.

I am working with my Daddy, and I am right beside Him. Whatever He needs me to do, I am here to learn and perform the duty with pleasure and honor.

Our focus is fueled again, and it is a mega push from Him to soar like never. I stand with a spirit of expectation and a heart full of love because He chose me. He set me free from bondage and sin. He gave me new life in Him. He touched my heart and renewed my passion for His heart. His deep speaks to my deep. I saw my little niece the other day just hanging on my brother, and she was just giggling and laughing. It is so beautiful when a girl knows she has her daddy.

She told him, "I'm a magnet on you, Daddy!" Wow, just thinking about it is so precious. That is how we are or should be with our heavenly Father. Wherever He goes, we go. Whatever He says, we say it with Holy Ghost boldness and strength.

His voice speaks through us, releasing the authority to call those things as though they were.

Such a powerful declaration for us to stand on and know in our hearts that we are loved tremendously. Everywhere my brother went, she was right there. This day, join me and declare the decree that we will be like a magnet to our heavenly Father. We walk with Him and work right alongside Him with fervor and grace. The funny thing is that we are the girly girls with the ability to reign with dominion and power. He blessed man and woman both with the authority and the power to reign over the fish, the birds, and every living thing that moves on the earth.

So, it is quite natural to work with my Daddy because I am fearfully and wonderfully made. I am made in His image. I look just like Him. I sound just like Him, and I love it. When we were younger and in our development stages, people would often say, you look just your mama and daddy. What a significant compliment.

They were prophesying to me what I would be doing and calling my future forward with the words of their mouth.

As I watched my niece with my brother, she knew her heart was protected with her daddy. She can call her daddy and know that he will do anything to protect her and guide her. He shows her how to read and study. Her daddy is her magnet, and she is his little magnet.

Pray with Me at This Moment

Heavenly Father, thank you for loving us and watching over us. We worship and adore You. Thank you for the Blood of Jesus and all the power it holds manifested in our lives. Forgive us for anything that may not have or did not properly line up with Your Word. We forgive anyone who may have done anything toward us. We bless You, and we declare the decree that we will walk in the newness of Christ and be the new creature You made us to be. May we be like magnets to You and cling to You with nothing in between.

Thank you for calling us Your own and creating in us the passion to be Your beautiful girls who have been transformed; you are your authentic, amazing, and uniquely designed abundant women. Thank you for healing our hearts from old hurts and pains, filling the voids of the past that tried to linger. Thank you that we are now walking into this new place of grace, and we fully embrace our special anointing as Your daughters. Thank you for the power to break forth and see the power of Your holy hand gingerly guiding us to the platform of the world to let them know we are Your little girl.

We stand with the Holy Ghost's boldness, and we shout it out loud that we are so God-proud. We have our hands up and open to receive as we stand with our faith to believe.

Order our steps strongly as we walk with the hinds' feet in high places according to your Holy Word in Psalm 18:33. Thank you for enlarging our territories and increasing our capacities to carry the glorious anointings. We pick up the mantles, and we take the Gospel of Jesus the Christ to the world and let everyone we meet know how You opened our eyes to see.

It is a new season, and you are the beautiful reason we can throw off the hurt little girl clothes and walk as an outstanding woman of God.

We let old broken promises be mended with the sure promises of You. You said Your promises are yes and amen. We run to the new place, the wide-open space, and laugh. We are now in this victorious, overcoming status. Thank you for Jesus allowing us to touch the hem of His garment so that we could receive the powerful healing in our spirit and soul so that we can possess fullness and walk in the light of You and be whole. Thank you for the gifts that You have imparted to us so that we could touch the world with the words given to us from You. It is You we stick to like glue. It is not like regular glue; it is a supernatural glue. Hallelujah!

Because we chose to stick to You, no one can pluck us out of Your hands. You have engraved us in the palm of Your hands, as You said in Isaiah 49:16. Thank you for your tender mercies and for loving us with an everlasting love.

We bless You for the Holy Spirit. Lead and guide us into all truth and knowledge. Thank you for releasing the mysteries of the Gospel, and we will always be the ones to give You all the glory and honor. We love You and thank You in Jesus Christ's name. Amen.

Now. Now She. Now Her. Now You. Now Me.

(1 Chronicles 7:20–24 NKJV)

Have you ever thought about the times when you have been praying about a particular matter or concern and wondered when you would see or get the answer? Better yet, you are in the midst of a new phase of your life, and it seems the details are a little vague, but you know in your spirit that something amazing is about to happen? Can you say, "Now!" Now is the powerful three-letter word that causes a shift in the atmosphere, literally. When you ask the question, when is it going to be what I need it to be? You can say, "Now," and instantly, the time changes to what you and I need it to be to accomplish the task or assignments.

The Holy Spirit is so powerfully extraordinary. He allows us to see exactly what we need to see when He is moving us into the next dimension and realm of His glory. It is when we can decide on purpose to speak the word "now." It is a pur-posed "now." The word that pushes us out of the past into our present, then at the same time sets us up for our future. Which, in that next moment, will be in our now. Jehovah is so strategic because He has so many blessings and special touches that He will make sure we are in the right position to receive and perceive it.

We have been looking outward at the environment, and we have crying out to Jehovah, then He says, "My darling little girl, I'm right here." Whenever you and I are crossing over into a new dimension and realm of revelation, it seems so dark and scary, yet it is beautiful and full of light. The enemy tried to put fear and cause us to want to stop and scream, but it is the opposite. We run and shout, "Hallelujah!" It is the highest praise. We have just turned the weapon of fear into a weapon of faith! Girls, do you see it? It is so outstanding; our supernatural extraordinary status has stood up in us because of the Holy Ghost.

Our heavenly Father declared we are engraved in the palm of His hand. Thank you, Jehovah, for rescuing us and placing us in the shadow of thy wing. We are protected and sheltered from the tactics of the enemy. Now. We can. Now. We must. Now. We move forward. Now. We capture. Indeed. Now.

Sometimes, when we are looking at the plans and ideas that have been released to us by the spirit of the Lord, we find ourselves picking up a strength like never before. Our hearts are refreshed, and we feel the push of the Holy Spirit. When everything is going on, and you feel like nothing is clear, that is when the Lord God releases the now. Wow! Do you hear that? He releases a new phase in our life to move forward out of obscurity.

He sets our feet in a new place of strength and on a stage of power. We draw closer to our God and let His Mighty Word guide us further on the road of purpose and destiny. Take out the prophetic notes that were spoken in the light and make sure our hearts hear them. Read it out loud and say it proud. We see the primary key to the map and begin to chart our way to the connections, appointments, and holy visitations of our personal assignments. So, you may be wondering what does the now of your purpose means? Let us talk about this one woman amid all these people outlined in her family. Yes, you are the one who has been singled out and chosen to do something great. Yes, you and I. Created for the unusual exploits.

This woman, Sheerah, in our focused scripture text of 1 Chronicles 7:24, accomplished something so powerful. It was so powerful that it had to be noted and made known what was done by her hands. Sheerah means Kinswoman. She is a woman of physical strength and prestige. Wow, this woman had enough resources to build two towns with the work of her hands and the financial status of her hands. Yes, Lord, I will build and give. Yes, what our heavenly Father is doing through us has to be known. We must show forth His works and His glory. As we say yes and walk in obedience to His Word, we start experiencing so many amazing and extraordinary supernatural moves of the Highest God. We are called and chosen to do the phenomenal and supernatural extraordinary.

We cannot just go into a place and see it as everyone else sees it. We must make a conscious choice to say, "Yes, Lord, I will do the greater and the over above." Our Jehovah God, our heavenly Father, is so amazing, and he is our *big* God.

Our capacity is beyond the norm, and every time we are given an assignment and given a mission, it is in our DNA to do it *big* and do it excellently. Sheerah in this scripture was so totally cool that before her name is the word, "now." Think about it. Selah. The word "now" is drawing attention to Sheerah and making us to think of it right now. Turning our eyes to the present, indicating that it is at this moment. It is something that was done beyond the normal process. Sheerah is known amongst all the people within her bloodline and what she had done was important enough to be noted. Now Sheerah. Put your name here: Now,_____. Yes, it is so. It is a promise that we are now.

Considering the background of her name and what it means to be Sheerah. Yes, her name was purposed before the beginning of time, and she was given an assignment to make a difference and make a mark. She had to make a sound in such a way that it would make many take notice. Lady Sheerah, Kinswoman, a female relative. Her name is known to be associated with having keen responsibility. It reminds me of another person who was sent to be our Kinsman Redeemer. Jesus came to build the upper and the lower lands. He came to make sure we would be able to make phenomenal steps and run through troops, as well as leap over walls. We are all modern-day Sheerahs. We stand and proclaim the one true name, Jesus the Christ. We arise and build, now.

Now faith is the substance. Now is the time to stand up and be counted. Now is my promised word from my heavenly Father. Now is how I walk it. I am my Father's daughter, and I am doing a new thing now! Shout with me! Say it with me! I am doing a new thing now. I, _____, am doing a new thing now. It may seem hard and overwhelming, but that is only the devil trying to stop you. You must push back and do it. Get up and do it now. Move past the old and look towards the new. The doldrums and sleepiness are removed so you and I can receive our now. During this time, our world is experiencing different things; however, we are still able to possess our now.

Sheerah built lower and upper Beth Horon (in Hebrew, the house of the freemen or freedom houses) and Uzzen Sheerah (in Hebrew, a remnant turning their face to hear God). Sheerah was walking like a boss lady before there were boss ladies.

Say this with me: "I am declaring today that I am walking in my boss lady status. My inheritance is a boss lady, and I receive it. My Daddy says it; I can do it."

Sheerah had accomplished major feats and was charted as a major player, a female player. What is so amazing about this is that it said she was his daughter. We are Jehovah's daughter. Let us break past the monotony of it all and do some outlandish and beyond the norm things. When people see us or hear our name, they say there she is. Did you know that she built a town? I hold the capacity to build a town. That is what I will do with the power of the Holy Ghost and the strength of the Lord God Jehovah. I am going for the upper and the lower. I arise and build a town with the Word of Jehovah God. I will go to the lower parts of the world and build them up so they can know they are loved and precious. I am a builder. I am a woman builder.

Did you know these lower parts of the world are right in our neighborhood? They are in our workplaces. These are the people working in the grocery stores and markets. The ones who have been downtrodden and cast down because of their past and walking in shame. But God! Hallelujah! We have all received a "but God" in our lives and were able to stand and proclaim the one true name. Now. We can go and help them. I will go to the upper parts of the world and let them know they are precious and they have a purpose. These are the ones who are famous and popular amongst the city and nations. They have all the material wealth; however, they are still needing the inner healing and hearts restored. Whether they are the upper or the lower parts, they are still needing the wholeness of the Blood of Jesus the Christ.

Then, it is recorded that Sheerah built Uzzen Sherrah. I believe this is consisting of the generations in her bloodline. Everyone who is connected to us by blood or marriage, or whether grafted in by friendship. We must look at our lineage tree and decide to break the barriers to have the overflow and the abundance in my life.

Uzzen in Hebrew, the remnant of people who are willing to turn their face to hear the sound. Sheerah was given the awesome assignment to build a house that would represent a place of the remnant can turn their faces to hear the Highest God and follow His Word. It is time for us to arise and build alongside our Father. We are to send the word out to those who are willing and to worship Jehovah and give praise to Jesus.

Our destiny guide, the Holy Bible, says in Matthew 5:16 to not hide our light. Too many times, we have hidden our light to please others, or we did not know that our light was being dimmed because of other things from the past. Take the light out and let it shine. Let it shine so bright that people will have to ask who is that lady or who is that girl? I am not backing down. I am releasing my sound. I am Brown Girl Rich!

Now. Now She. Now Her. Now You. Now Me.

Not giving up, not giving out, not giving in! Just walking in my God-given authority. I am "His daughter," and I am doing it like my Daddy. In Jesus, the Christ name! Now His daughter, Karen. Amen now, His daughter, you. Amen.

"I Declare the Decree. I Prophesy"

(Acts 21:9 NKJV)

I shall have what I decree. I am called and chosen to do the greater. Jesus said that I will do the greater because He went to the Father. He is in me, and my heavenly Father is in me. Therefore, I have the greater One in me, and He is doing great things in me. I declare the decree of John 14:11–14. It is time to stand and proclaim the name above all names, Jesus the Christ name. When I walk around the town, I can help someone's heart. They can see there is more that they can achieve. I open my mouth and prophesy.

It had been a while since I had declared the words that had been given to me by my heavenly Father. I was walking around wondering and wandering. I was wondering who, what, when, where, and why things were different and not what I was thinking. In as much also, I was wandering around in someone else's words. One day, the Holy Ghost spoke to my heart. He gingerly held me close and whispered in my ear something so true and sweet. He said, "If you are going to receive something different, then you are going to have to say something totally opposite of what you are seeing and saying."

You see, I was saying what others were declaring over my life. My walk was not in tune with the Word of God. So, I took a few minutes, got on my knees, and repented. I decided that I wanted what Jehovah God has for me. My heart felt rejuvenated, and my soul was refreshed. I took the Word of God and started to speak it out over my life. Things started to shift and take shape into purposeful manifestation. I realized that I needed to open my mouth and prophesy what thus saith the Lord. The words of my mouth and my meditations were going to have to line up and be in direct alignment to speak what He has already said.

Especially before I was formed in my mother's womb. These prophetic and apostolic words are so important in how we function and walk in our purpose and destiny.

In the Book of Acts, there was one man named Phillip, who had four daughters who were virgins and prophetesses. The interesting thing about this scripture is that these girls were mentioned once, and they are called virgins, without a doubt packing the Word. They have a purity and a strength like none other. A person walking in virginity has the capacity to walk with a relationship with the Lord and have an amazing communion with the Father. There is nothing in the way of their thought processes and the way they can communicate the truths.

The mere fact they are prophetesses indicates they had a relationship with the Father and were filled with the spirit of the Lord. These women were called Phillip's daughters. Their names were not shared in the passage, and no one knows their names; however, we know who they are and what they stood for without a doubt. A virgin makes a stand for purity and holds a stance of commitment.

We can consider the two words in the sentence that said they symbolize a connection with their purity and the Word of God. Our heavenly Father's love for us is so pure and true. When He chose us, He knew exactly what He wanted and how He wanted those gifts to be magnified. It is an honor to be called His daughter. We have such a treasure in just being called "daughter." It is a relationship thing. When my mom says, "my daughter," it is so beautiful to hear it and see our pictures reflect who is in the natural resemblance, and our mannerisms are highlighted. Then, when we come into the realization of being called our "father's daughter." We are instantly noted as belonged. We are not lost; we are not without a bloodline or history.

It is our father's last name that gives us ours sense of direction and purpose of who we are. Our father's legacy and history are our map and plan.

When we gravitate to our heavenly Father's Word, it solidifies who we are in every sense of the way. We know who we are, and we have so much to offer.

Our hearts and spirits are connected to our father, and we have an inner guide with the Holy Spirit who makes sure we do not get off track.

Our DNA matches our daddies, and we are uniquely designed to speak and prophesy everything we need to come to pass. We do not have to worry about who we are and where we came from. These virgin prophetesses were put there for a reason. They were serving with their daddy in doing the work of the Lord. What an honor! Yes, Lord, we will serve with You. We will serve Your people and make sure the Word is prophesied with honor and truth in purity. Thank you for giving us our identity. We are affirmed every time we look in your Word, and we see ourselves as in a mirror. We are fearfully and wonderfully made, and we know it full well. Hallelujah!

Pray with me: Father God, we thank you for who You are and how You created us in Your image. Thank you for our perfect DNA. We honor and bless Your holy name. May our steps be orchestrated, and our hearts be divinely knitted with Yours, so we walk in divine order. Our ears are turned and tuned to Your voice.

Let our hands be in Your hands as we do the work and serve in faith, with the Holy Spirit. There are many things out there, but we know that Your true pure Word will guide us, and we are able to succeed at what we are commissioned to do. We will prophesy and declare the decree, Your Word.

It is an honor, and we thank you for calling and choosing us. We ask for forgiveness for not totally surrendering at times; however, we are here at Your feet to receive the good thing. We are here to hear and flow in the anointing of Your loving Holy Spirit. Beautiful are the feet of those who carry Your Word. Thank you. In Jesus the Christ name, amen.

"Jehovah God Said Us Too!"

(Joel 2:28–29, NKJV)

"Go ahead; you can do it too!" I love this phrase in the passage according to Joel 2:28–29, as we are given the declared promise of our heavenly Father. He says He will pour His Spirit on all flesh; your sons and daughters shall prophesy, the older men are going to dream, and young men shall see visions. This is where I see my name and your name as a woman of our heavenly Father. He also says, my men who serve me and my maids who serve me. The maidservants of the Lord God! We are they! Hallelujah!

When we were younger, and there was an opportunity to go to an event or receive a special treat, it always seemed like the boys were the only ones who could go or get it. Well, we girls would always run to daddy and ask can we have it too, or can we go? Some things are meant just for boys, and there are some things meant just for girls. The fashion industry has generated trillions of dollars catering to the specific gender of clothing and colors. In fact, some items need to be just for men and some just specifically for girls. I love my curves, curlies, colors, and special fragrant perfumes.

They fit my curves just for me, and I am glad about it.

However, when it comes to anointings, prophecies, callings, purposes, and destinies, The Lord God has specifically laid it out. He said He is releasing dreams and visions to the old and young men, as well as his menservants. But then, this is where is He tells us to stand at attention and receive. We are the hand-maidens, the maidservants; the "let be unto me according to your word" crew.

Ladies, grab your dresses, pretty shoes, and look cute while we declare thus saith the Lord God with Holy Ghost boldness! I love it! I do not have to look hard and rugged to preach it or declare the decrees! I can because my Daddy said I can. We can go into the places and help someone get closer to Christ and not be afraid of them looking at us weird. It is our time, and we are chosen for such a time as this. Can you see that I am excited? It is because I am so excited and thrilled that I can walk in the unfriendly environment and change its climate because I am indeed a "climate changer."

When the Lord God chose me before the foundation of this world, He knew I would need extra courage and Holy Ghost boldness to make a shift in the atmosphere with my voice. Not afraid to say it loud and proud that I am in love with Jesus. I am a lover of worship music and, most of all, the Word of God. Sisters, regardless of your skin color and size of your jeans, get up and at it. Let's do it, together we can!

We have work to do. No more sitting in the corner being afraid. Grab another sister and tell her and tell her, let us do this right.

The purpose of the call and the anointing upon us is to make a difference and be a difference among many. So many times, we have been distracted by emotions, actions of others, words, fears, dreads, cares of the world, and everything that would look real but was an imitation. Our heavenly Father is real, and we are in His image. Now that we have seen where we were lagging or just slow, it is time to pick up the pace. You know, increase the speed and get rid of the need to be pleasing somebody.

Yes, I said it! Women get in the rut of waiting on the word "go" from someone when our Daddy has already said go from the start. I see why He said to lay aside every weight in Hebrews 12:1 (NKJV). That weight can be any type of sin. The sin of not receiving His love and looking for it in every place but the right place. The place is in your heart. He loves us with an everlasting love, and His love is like a banner over us. We are covered, sealed, healed, loved, and refreshed all with His love. What an awesome gift from the best Giver. Receive it this day! Open it and let it be the best dress you clothe yourself in, along with your full armor. Let it be the best fragrance or perfume we wear. Let it be what people see or hear every time we are in their presence. It is His presence we want to see and hear. Yes, it is so.

It will exude from us like a fresh wind flowing from heaven. Yes, it may have been hard to realize it, but His love is going to remove the pain that you have been carrying around for years.

Agree with me and know in your heart that the anointing that is on us is unique and sweet. We have it, and we can do it with the cuteness and the boldness because our Daddy said we can. In Jesus, the Christ name, amen!

"She, You, Me, We Take Territory"

(Joshua 17:6 NKJV)

There is a famous slogan that everyone uses, and it is sometimes taken to be casual. However, when someone says, "Give me my stuff, or I'm going to get my stuff," it usually means that it is about to be a throwdown. Well, that is exactly what is going on with this daughter. What is interesting is that these daughters do not have to say anything; it is stated in the passage of scripture that they are automatically counted in as receivers of land.

When I think of this scenario, I am giving the heavenly Father the glory because it is such a reminder to us that we have already been given blessed portions of land. When we think of land, it is generally a large section of ground or property that can be used for various uses. Spiritually, land can represent authority, a segmented piece set aside for a specific purpose.

The territory we are given is for us to build, plant, uproot, develop, and cultivate. We are taking land and creating something different. Our hands are anointed to do it and accomplish what is visually unique and representative of our heavenly Father. Most of the time, when someone is given something, if they are not aware of its value, they will abuse or misuse it. In this case, when the daughters are given land, it does not say what they used the land for, but it was indicated they were to take their property and drive out the enemy. Let us think of our families, careers, and communities. We are to take the land and drive out the enemy. Our kingdom assignment is to take the land and transform it to the glory of God. Ladies, we are not just called to get the property and sit on it as a little house with the common picket fence. Let us take the land we are given in our purview and make a difference.

We see that young teenage girl and help her through a difficult time. We see that young child and guide them through their growth phases. The very moment someone comes around us, we are given the opportunity to pluck up the weeds, pull down the strongholds, and plant the seeds of Jehovah's Word and share the Gospel of Jesus the Christ. Allow the Holy Ghost to share the plans of Jehovah God and provide a safe place for someone to learn about Jesus and show them the love of Christ.

Territory, what are you doing with it? I asked myself that same question. Heavenly Father gives us territory every day, and we could make something happen with it. A powerful revelation and truth were shared with me.

In the middle of the names be shown who had what territory, Manasseh's daughters were significantly placed in the names to show that it mattered that these girls were to own property. The interesting part of the ownership of the territory is that Manasseh's name means that Jehovah God caused Joseph to forget his troubles. Today, we can take that same promise for ourselves. Our heavenly Father loves us so much, and He will make sure we do not have any issues.

We are victorious with any territory assignment He gives us. When the enemy tries to come in, the Holy Ghost will lift a standard against him. I am always reminded of how Jeremiah, in chapter 1, was named a prophet from his mother's womb and was given the most delicate yet powerful mission to take the land, throw down, uproot, plant, pull-up, and tear down, to build, to plant. We are put in charge of nations and kingdoms. The scenario of the land is the person's heart, mind, soul, and spirit we must go in according to 2 Corinthians 10:4–6, that strongholds are pulled down.

Like vines growing in trees, we must cut them off at the root before they start growing and trying to overtake the nature of something beautiful. Every negative seed must be plucked up, and the seed of Jehovah's Word must be planted. Let the Holy Spirit water it so that it can receive the supernatural increase.

We may have the assignment of planting or watering. Whichever one it is, only Jehovah God will give the increase. Our purpose calls us to a higher plan, and that is not to consider just our land but to tend to the fields that we are assigned to bring forth much harvest. According to Psalm 110:1, it is time for us to rule amid our enemies. Ladies, according to Isaiah 60:1 in The Message Bible, he puts emphasis on getting up out of the bed, wake up and put our faces in the sunshine. Shine on us, oh Lord!! In Jesus the Christ name, amen.

She Said to Herself

She said to herself: Matthew 9:20–22 (121 times in the Bible), referring to herself, meaning she had to decide within her heart!

No one could do this for her; she was going to have to get up and go.

Make a move and say, self, it is time for a change.

She had been a secret place for a long time, praying for a change to come, but this time, it was going to come from within herself.

She says to herself.

This time, I will push forward and do what needs to be done to get my healing. I heard about Jesus, and I have seen everyone else reach out and touch him.

When they touch him, they get healed?

When they touch him, they are made new?

When they touch him, they are not the same?

So, self, here I go, I am pushing through,

Yes, I just hear them saying—"What is she doing? Who

does she think she is? Where did she come from? Why doesn't someone stop her?"

Self, keep moving, keep going, do not listen to them, keep focused, Jesus is in town, and this time, _____, I am going to be healed, I am going to keep walking in honor, I am royalty, I heard the word when they said that he multiplied fish and bread and fed the multitudes!

Surely, he can heal me if I just touch him.

Just got to get to him! I wonder if I ask can I go up there near him will they let me; that is okay, they will not understand!

I will touch him; I will touch him,

I heard when they said that we are His children, heirs to the kingdom.

So, that means I am entitled, and that is already mine. So, here goes, keep pushing.

Sure are a lot of people here; that is okay; they all have different needs, but not like my needs. I must keep moving.

I cannot let anything get in my way, not even that man that said that he cared, not the fact that the bills are piled high, family acting up, and to think they didn't want to come with me. Whatever, Jesus is in town and today is my day.

No longer do I just sit and wait for him to come to my door; I am going to him.

If I could just touch his hem! I do not need to get him to say anything because everybody wants to talk to him. I remember that it was said that he would have healing in his wings. Well, I just want to touch him a little bit.

I know what, I will go low, if I stand up, everybody will push me, but if I go low, no one will see me, and then I can get to him quicker, yes, that is it! Stay low and believe.

Well, self, let's do it, let us go low, let's worship, let me pray, let me praise, let me sit at his feet. I want what he wants for me, and that is to be made whole.

That is it, wow, everybody up there reaching to touch his arms and get his attention, and I am already at his feet. Here goes!

If I could just touch the hem, it will work; yes, it will work. Yes! I did it! I touched his hem, and it was wonderful! I feel something happening! What is going on in me? I am changing! I feel a smile is on my face! Oh, my goodness, Jehovah, what just happened. You said if I believe, it will happen for me.

Okay, girl, get it together; you just got healed but cannot be too loud; take it slow, breathe, keep moving, so you can get to the tent! They will be surprised when they see the new me! Oh yes, I will keep it to myself because they will not believe it. Okay, let us go!

Wait!! Who touched me! (Oh my, is he talking to me? How could he know that it was me? I stayed at feet as low as I could) okay, I will turn around—be calm and cool. See what he has to say.

"Daughter, be encouraged! Your faith has made you well!"

And the woman was healed at that moment. (At once) instantly. Wow! It has happened after all these years, I am healed, and it only took a step of faith! Just staying at his feet and making a move to him! Thank you! I am whole—happy, healthy, restored, and full of a new day! Ladies—we are all daughters!— this time, we walk in blessing, healing, God's spirit; this time, we recognize and honor the gift that has been placed on the inside of each of us!

We are treasures. This time, we walk in renewed life—the old things have passed away, we are new creatures. This time, we walk in our nobility—we are royalty—we are the king's daughters and sisters of faith.

We come from the north, south, east, and west—the four corners of the earth to speak to nations all over! We can rule and reign—this time, we say to ourselves, we make decrees, declarations, and proclamations that will shape worlds and tear down structures that have been inside of our world for too long.

She was dealing with her issue for twelve years, and she said to herself! Enough is enough! Today, decide within yourself; enough is enough!

Wise woman! Arise and walk in love, use your faith, use your key to fan the flame of another sister so she may stay focused on Christ as she moves in her purpose and destiny!

We are powerful! We are wise women working our faith!

Hallelujah! Hallelujah!

I Am Woman: Daughter

I am my Father's daughter!

I am the apple of His eye!

He loves me with an everlasting love!

He sings songs of deliverance over me!

I am blessed and favored with His love!

My Father has called me into light from darkness.

I am a daughter of Zion.

I walk in the inheritance of His Word.

I am a woman of faith in action.

I am made whole by His touch.

My faith makes me whole.

I reconcile others to Him.

My steps are ordered and orchestrated daily.

I am chosen for such a time as this.

I am fearfully and wonderfully made.

I walk in the beauty of His holiness.

I am made rich by Him.

I call Him Abba.

He has fashioned and knitted me in my mother's womb. He knew me before forming me.

I am His handmaiden, and I say let it be done according to thy Word.

His favor surrounds me as a shield.

His spirit is poured out upon me.

I prophesy and call forth.

I declare and decree things, and they are established!

I have keys of the kingdom to bind and to loosen.

I agree with His word spoken over my life and those that are connected to me.

I am clothed with His armor.

I am covered by the Blood of Jesus.

I am daily loaded with benefits.

The Holy Spirit leads and guides me daily.

As a daughter, I am a joint heir with my big brother Jesus.

I can dream dreams and visions.

I press towards the mark of a higher calling.

Dear Daddy

I can speak what He speaks.

I am created in my Father's image

I am more than a conqueror.

I call those things to be not as though they were.

He has given me grace gifts for His glory.

I walk with the sword of the Spirit in my hand.

My feet are like hinds' feet—I can go in high places.

I trust my Father and am still. I know He is God.

He reveals the secret things to me.

Hidden riches are mine because of my inheritance.

The Word of God is hidden in my heart.

Purity is my covenant right.

I am designed for a purpose, and I have a covenant mate.

I am anointed for special assignments.

I am in my wealthy place, and I am in overflow perpetually.

I look like my Daddy; I sound like my Daddy; I do what my Daddy does.

I am filled with His Spirit.

I am blessed among women.

I walk in the excellence in everything I do.

Every place the soles of my feet tread, I possess the land.

I speak to nations—I can change the atmosphere.

I am a money magnet—I generate wealth—I help build and finance the kingdom.

The power of the Holy Spirit operates inside of me.

My Father is rich!

He is Holy; therefore, I am holy.

I am blessed with all spiritual blessings.

I am the seed of Abraham.

He hides me in the shadow of His wings.

His favor goes before me.

I am chosen by my Father.

The presence of the Lord is mine.

I have a unique sound that is recognized by my Father.

I am my Father's daughter.

I have special gifts and treasures that are used for His glory.

My tents are big, and my territories are enlarged.

The glory of the Lord has risen upon me.

The Spirit of the Lord is upon me.

My enemies are my footstool.

I am an encourager, and I go out to share the Gospel.

I am my Father's daughter. I am a woman! I am loved! I Am My Father's Daughter!

Arise (You've Got Work to Do)

In Worship, Prophecy Comes

Enter another dimension of worship, prayer, intercession, declaring, decreeing—seeing it happen quickly. Natural time does not match the Kairos timing! Receive it! Watch Kairos time take place in matters of the heart. Those things that are concerning you and those around you. It is happening quicker and sooner than you thought. Dreams and visions coming to past! The power of the Holy Ghost directing the dreams and visions. It is our duty to come forth! The dreams and visions were listening to the past and what others had spoken, but now they are under the move of the Holy Spirit. When you speak, the dreams and visions are going to list and manifest. Hallelujah!

Conceive and conceive again and conceive again! When you birth out! Conceive again! Always evolve! Always emerge! Keep emerging to the new and blessed you! He is with us! Always go forth!

***

New wine! This kind is vintage—(being the best of its kind, the wine from a particular harvest, choice, an exceptionally fine wine from the crop of a good year). It has been sitting in the cellar for a long time; now it is to be brought forth—to release the scent of the fragrance of the new wine—just like when the wine connoisseur sniffs it to sense its value and worth, as well as its aging. This aging was for a period to be brought so others may taste its goodness!

It will be poured forth as a taste like no other. Many will drink this new wine. They will say, "Where has this wine been?" They will ask for more! They will know that it has been held for just this moment!

Note: when wine has been in the cellar—it has been stored in a dark, dry place to protect its sealing. Most of the time, when one is going through that dry, dark time, it is easy to wonder what is going on or are you hearing God, but now is the time for the cork to be popped for a fresh new taste of His goodness and love. The waiting you experienced in the cellar prepared you for the unveiling and revealing in the upper room. You waited, and you held on, so now experience the light of His love and power. He is pouring forth a special touch that only you can feel.

Each bottle of fine wine has a special label describing the year it was stored. As the wine connoisseur says, "It is a good year." Regardless of what may have happened in the past, you are good. You are blessed! You are anointed! You are talented! You are gifted! You are a "good year"! Hallelujah!

So, woman. Arise! So, man! Arise and come to the light and feel His warmth. Arise and come to the place where He has called you! Come to the place where He will speak to you and call you out of the old into the new. Arise! Arise! Come forth! Wake up! Arise! Get up! Arise! Stand up! Arise! You are needed! Arise! You have a purpose! Arise! You have a destiny! Arise! You are loved! Arise! Arise! Arise! Receive the mantle of a unique gift and calling! Arise! Take it and wear it! Arise! Walk in it! Arise! It is time to arise!

Purpose[1]

Wine cellars protect alcoholic beverages from potentially harmful external influences, providing darkness and a constant temperature. Wine is a natural, perishable food product.

 Left exposed to heat, light, vibration, or fluctuations in temperature and humidity, all types of wine can spoil. When safely stored, wines not only maintain their quality, but many improve in aroma, flavor, and complexity as they mature.

Even though it may have felt like a long time during the wait, every situation and circumstance only help make you a good wine! Bless Jehovah! The scent, the taste, and the uniqueness of how Jehovah God made each one is so awesome! Arise! Be good wine!

 Amen.

Find Your Smile — 10-15-09, 4:41 p.m.

Find your smile when you thought it was hiding under so many hurts. It is there because it was given to you and it has such beautiful worth. The Lord God knew the things that you would face and go through so you can relax. Find your smile when you are hurting in a way you never thought you would experience. Maybe he did not choose you, maybe it was not the right business deal, no, they were not the right best friend, but there is one He would send.

Find your smile deep down inside of your heart. Think of the joyous times when you had that hot chocolate on the cold nights, the popcorn and the pillow fights, the fresh moments of bubble baths and long showers. Find your smile when you see the pretty roses, birds, and those different types of flowers. Rolling in the grass and seeing the clouds change from pillow puffs to cotton balls to birds to butterflies; either way, you are walking in the new and getting rid of the old ties. You are on a new escapade of life's beautiful experiences; you can laugh, love, and hold.

Your smile is the avenue to put on the new garments and discard the old. Find your smile in the family that you thought was so far away; they never left you, nor did you leave them.

It was a figment of the imagination that made it bigger than it was. Your smile is in the friends that were specifically put out of sight so you could find the real you.

You are special, and you have something special inside of you. So, find your smile and let it shine like never before. Let it bring joy to you and others. It is so amazing what your smile will do. It causes your eyes to smile and your spirit to smile. Your smile is connected to other smiles. Your smile starts someone else to smile, and it takes away the pain of what was and moves them to what is and what could be.

My love, find your smile, look inside, and speak to it. Release it because it has been hidden so long behind the tears of yesterday's past. It has been hiding behind the loves that did not last. You might as well let it out because it has been waiting on you to tell it that it is connected to joy! It is a contagious joy! It cannot be stopped, stifled, or put out. It is a smile generated by the Spirit of the living God! Hold on to the vision, the dreams, the desires, and the inner thoughts that sparkle. You are a unique person, and your ability to touch awaits the hands, the hearts, the spirits, the eyes, and the love of others.

Sweet one, find your smile; it is there to give light to the dark places of the soul.

It can heal without saying a word, and your smile can represent a sweet melody that has never been heard.

Find your smile!

Confessions of a Daughter

I Am My Father's Daughter

I do what He does, I say what He says, I see what He says, I have what He says I am more than a conqueror, I am the head and not the tail, I walk in victory in every area of my life, I am anointed, I am appointed, I am equipped for such a time as this, I have a hope, I have a calling, I have a purpose, I have a destiny, I walk in obedience, I am willing, I eat the good of the land, I am a woman of virtue, I am a woman of truth, a woman of love, a woman of purity, my needs are met! I am blessed with all spiritual blessings, I am loved, I am fearfully and wonderfully made—fearfully, and wonderfully made for a specific walk. My mate is blessed and covered by the Blood of Jesus the Christ! my heart is pure; my life is blessed! I have the blessing in my life. I am wealthy- I have the ability and power to get wealth!

I am prospering in everything I set my hands to do. My feet are anointed to go in high places! I have feet dipped in oil anointed to tread on scorpions and serpents and not get hurt! I am a woman who loves one man. Sickness and poverty have no place in my life. Lack and slack must flee right now. I attract money. I attract the best; I wear the best; I eat the best.

I have the best of everything. I am the King's daughter! I have an inheritance. I am beautiful! I am unique! I am obedient! I eat the good of the land. My needs are daily met! I have a new outlook. I have the mind of Christ. I think of things that are beautiful, lovely, good report, and praiseworthy.

I hold the thoughts and purposes of His heart. I walk in the sure steps. I have a wealthy place. The Lord God is my Father! I have a special view of what the Father shows me. Sweet treats are mine.

Holy Spirit guides me into all spiritual wisdom, truth, and revelation. Holy Spirit is my comforter, and He reveals the truth! I am in the right covenant relationship. My home is blessed, and I can provide for others. Jehovah God is my Provider; He meets all my needs and gives me the desires of my heart. I lean not to my own understanding; I acknowledge the Lord in all my ways! He directs my paths! He anoints my eyes to see a fresh vision and new ideas. I have witty ideas and inventions! He opens doors for me that no one else can open. He closes doors for me that no one else can open. He is my Father, and I am His daughter. In Jesus the Christ name, amen.

The Treasure in Me

Please Say This Out Loud to Yourself and Let Your Spirit Hear and Agree With It!

I am a treasure and full of the Holy Ghost, and I am not to be compared! I am unique! I am blessed! And I was created with purpose!

Now call a sister and tell them: "Sister, you are a treasure, you are full of the Holy Ghost, and you are not to be compared! You are unique! You are blessed! And you were created with purpose!"

Now let us be jewels together in God's treasure chest!

Hallelujah! Praise our heavenly Father.

Pray and sing! A lot of times, people try to compare the treasures that are amongst us, but when you are unique, you cannot be compared.

So, we celebrate each other and shine as we glow together. Amen!

In a treasure chest, you see all sorts of jewels and special stones, you see the colors of splendor, majesty, and they all seem to have their shine individually,

But, oh, when they get together! You may have to put your shades on!

Where is the shine coming from? Whether it is the diamond! The ruby! The turquoise! The garnet! The sapphire! The amethyst!

You just cannot tell! So today, as we walk with purpose, we can shine individually and collectively without outshining each other. Wow! So awesome!

Hallelujah!

Afflicted city, storm-battered, unpitied: I'm about to rebuild you with stones of turquoise, Lay your foundations with sapphires, construct your towers with rubies, Your gates with jewels, and all your walls with precious stones. All your children will have God for their teacher—what a mentor for your children! You'll be built solid, grounded in righteousness, far from any trouble—nothing to fear! Far from terror—it won't even come close! If anyone attacks you, don't for a moment suppose that I sent them, And if any should attack, nothing will come of it. I create the blacksmith who fires up his forge and makes a weapon designed to kill. I also create the destroyer—but no weapon that can hurt you has ever been forged. Any accuser who takes you to court will be dismissed as a liar. This is what God's servants can expect. I'll see to it that everything works out for the best. God's Decree.

Isaiah 54:11–17 (MSG)

That means God said it, and He means it.

So, you can rest assured that you are blessed and that the things that tried to hurt you are broken this day! You are a treasure that cannot be compared.

It is your heritage to be healed, and no weapon can harm you—no weapon of debt, lack, fear, distrust, evil words spoken, or thoughts someone may have thought.

You are a woman walking with purpose, and you can move forward knowing that your steps are ordered!

Example: If you walk with the compass—you cannot get off track, but just in case you do feel like you are needing some reassurance, just pull out your compass and go north! It always points north!

North is the Father!—Get in your worship! Get in your praise! Get in your fasting! Get in your solitude with Him and watch Him guide you!

So, woman with purpose!—you've got to always keep your compass! Holy Spirit, guide me.

Holy Spirit, lead me! Holy Spirit, hold me!

When you are walking with purpose! You are containing a weapon that cannot be seen or taken away!

A treasure:[2] defined as wealth or riches stored or accumulated in the form of precious metals, money, or jewels. Also, it is anything or person greatly valued or highly prized. To treat as precious or cherish.

A treasure: defined as our Father's statement is you are chosen, set aside, a holy nation, a royal priesthood!

A Future in God

So roll up your sleeves, put your mind in gear,
be totally ready to receive the gift that is coming
when Jesus arrives. Do not lazily slip back into
those old grooves of evil, doing just what you feel
like doing. You did not know any better than; you
do now. As obedient children, let yourselves be
pulled into a way of life shaped by God's life, a
life energetic and blazing with holiness. God said,
'I am holy; you be holy.'

1 Peter 1:13–16 (MSG)

"Clean house! Make a clean sweep of malice and pretense,
envy, and hurtful talk. You have had a taste of God. Now, like
infants at the breast, drink deep of God's pure kindness. Then
you will grow up mature and whole in God" (1 Peter 2:3–12,
MSG).

The Stone

Welcome to the living Stone, the source of life.
The workmen took one look and threw it out; God
set it in the place of honor. Present yourselves as
building stones for the construction of a sanctuary
vibrant with life, in which you will serve as holy
priests offering Christ-approved lives up to God.
The Scriptures provide precedent: Look! I am set-

ting a stone in Zion, a cornerstone in the place of honor. Whoever trusts in this stone as a foundation will never have cause to regret it. To you who trust him, he is a Stone to be proud of, but to those who refuse to trust him, The stone the workmen threw out is now the chief foundation stone. For the untrusting it is...a stone to trip over, a boulder blocking the way. They trip and fall because they refuse to obey, just as predicted. But you are the ones chosen by God, chosen for the high calling of priestly work, chosen to be a holy people, God's instruments to do his work and speak out for him, to tell others of the night-and-day difference he made for you—from nothing to something, from rejected to accepted. Friends, this world is not your home, so do not make yourselves cozy in it. Do not indulge your ego at the expense of your soul. Live an exemplary life among the natives so that your actions will refute their prejudices. Then they will be won over to God's side and be there to join in the celebration when he arrives.

1 Peter 2:3–12 (MSG)

So, here we are looking at these scriptures and see that the writer is saying, put away all the things that try to dull your luster! You are a jewel! You are a living stone! You are chosen for great work! You can move into a whole new dimension now! The things you do and the words you say are for God's glory and not man's story! Let your speech give life, and let your life give a speech to the things that are being a blessing to others!

Chosen: selected from several, preferred.

Elect: (of God) means to be selected for a divine mercy or favor, worthy to be chosen, to be received, favor of.

Purpose: The reason for which something exists or is made for! The true intended or desired result.

Woman: Created by our heavenly Father to aid or help! To uniquely crafted for a specific purpose.

With: Purposed and chosen to host; to contain; to possess; to consists of; to carry, be a vessel; to hold; to have additional circumstance; accompanied; connection to; in conjunction; joined with; hooked up with; union; in possession of!

Meanwhile, the moment we get tired in the waiting, God's Spirit is right alongside helping us along. If we do not know how or what to pray, it does not matter. He does our praying in and for us, making prayer out of our wordless sighs, our aching groans. He knows us far better than we know ourselves, knows our pregnant condition, and keeps us present before God. That is why we can be so sure that every detail in our lives of love for God is worked into something good.

God knew what he was doing from the very beginning. He decided from the outset to shape the lives of those who love him along the same lines as the life of his Son. The Son stands first in the line of humanity he restored. We see the original and intended shape of our lives there in him.

After God made that decision of what his children should be like, he followed it up by calling people by name. After he called them by name, he set them on a solid basis with himself. And then, after getting them established, he stayed with them to the end, gloriously completing what he had begun.

Romans 8:28–30 (MSG)

So, when you are walking with purpose, you make a conscious choice not to entertain foolishness: you choose the places you go; your choice is supposed to be in your inner circle. You make a choice to serve the Lord God!

You are full to the overflow! When you are walking with purpose! Nothing else can come in!—Even while you are being transformed!

The butterfly!—Knows its purpose! one of the few insects I know that will be consumed with purpose through the metamorphosis stage!

Holy Spirit, speak!

The natural water fountain!—Knows its purpose!—Cannot be filled with anything else; it keeps flowing and flowing! You cannot contain it. It is doing what it is created to do! You are a fountain flowing—you just keep doing what God has called you to do! Nothing can stop your flow! You are a worshipper! You worship! You keep worshipping—you keep praising, you keep serving! You keep giving! You keep loving.

As you keep going! You are replenished each time! You just flow; you are like the spring in a garden! You are saturated! You are nurtured! You help bring increase! Your water brings the nutrients that other need! Be purposed; contain purpose! Be an answer to someone! Be a blessing to someone!

Abraham walked with purpose—Isaac walked with purpose—Joseph walked with purpose! David walked with purpose! Jesus! Oh, he was just purpose!

You are fashioned and formed for greatness (Psalm 139:13–14).

The New Living Translation says, "You made all the delicate inner parts of my body and knitted me together in my mother's womb." Thank you for making me so wonderfully complex! Your workmanship is marvelous—how well I know it.

> For You did form my inward parts; You did knit me together in my mother's womb. I will confess and praise You for You are fearful and wonderful and for the awful wonder of my birth! Wonderful are Your works, and that my inner self knows right well. My frame was not hidden from You when I was being formed in secret [and] intricately and curiously wrought [as if embroidered with various colors] in the depths of the earth [a region of darkness and mystery].

Psalm 139:13–15 (AMP)

Fashioned means to shape and make; created, intricately designed, curiously wrought!

So here you are *woman—woman!*—Contained in purpose and encapsulated with the fullness of God!

W: Worshipper

O: Oracle

M: Multifaceted

E: Empowered and anointed

N: Nations birthed from her

1.Worshipper

A time will come, however, indeed it is already here, when the true (genuine) worshipers will worship the Father in spirit and in truth (reality); for the Father is seeking just such people as these as His worshipers. God is a Spirit (a spiritual Being) and those who worship Him must worship Him in spirit and in truth (reality). The woman said to Him, I know that Messiah is coming, He Who is called the Christ (the Anointed One); and when He arrives, He will tell us everything we need to know and make it clear to us. Jesus said to her, I Who now speak with you am He.

John 4:23-26 (AMP)

Operating in spirit and truth! She is a swat woman—serving authority and truth! She can hear the name Jesus and get into a praise! The woman at the well had all kinds of stuff going on, but when she learned of the living water! She had to tell somebody about who we are supposed to worship and how we are supposed to worship!

A woman who worships is a woman who loves!

Chosen to worship, a royal priesthood, a holy nation, peculiar people—offering up sacrifices and praises unto him!

Mary—began to burst forth in song after getting a word from the angel of the Lord.

"Then Mary took a pound of very costly oil of spikenard, anointed the feet of Jesus, and wiped His feet with her hair. And the house was filled with the fragrance of the oil" (John 12:3).

The Woman—New dimensions, new paths! Quantum leaps of His power! Of His glory!

2. Oracle (Luke 2:38)

The Handmaiden of the Lord.

Mary says, "Let it Be to Me according to thy word."

And you shall know, understand, and realize that I am in the midst of Israel and that I the Lord am your God and there is none else. My people shall never be put to shame. And afterward I will pour out My Spirit upon all flesh; and your sons and your daughters shall prophesy, your old men shall dream dreams, your young men shall see visions. Even upon the menservants and upon the maidservants in those days will I pour out My Spirit.

Joel 2:27-29 (AMP)

The woman can prophesy and make declarations to change the world.

The woman is multifaceted! She is like a ring—a diamond or a brilliantly cut jewel.

3. Multifaceted—means many ways and many sides, but she is a whole woman!

(Psalm 139:13–16)

She may have been hurt many times, but those things caused her to be strong, unique, and beautiful.

The woman can operate in many tasks but still be one whole woman!—A mama, a wife, a preacher, a teacher, a doctor, a gardener, and intercessor! Many ways! Many ways!

So, you look at the diamond—whether it is marquise, the emerald-shaped diamond-brilliant cut, the princess cut, regardless, has fifty-eight facets! Many sides to it, but they still can shine and reflect the light.

It does not matter how many times they talk about you, treat you bad or neglect you! Just shine and reflect the light!

You may have some rough times, but the cuts and bruises made you beautiful, and the opulence of who you are cannot be compared! Opulence—you are walking with abundance and richly supplied—inside and out.

The multi-faceted woman has brilliance about her! She has brightness, extreme radiance, great intelligence, ability, and skill.

Splendor, luster, shine, and excellence, clarity, agility, luminous!

Praise Jesus!

Anyway, the light hits her; she will shine with beautiful colors!

4. Empowered and anointed—(Genesis 2:18) Able to do what she needs to.

Anointed to walk in dominion. Authority, power, fashioned to fit, created to heal by laying hands on the sick, they recover, to call those things to be not as though they were, to call, to anoint, to pray and intercede, to stand in the gap, to give life, give birth! You are a woman! Able to contain, to pack, to host, to indwell, you are full of capacity!

Woman walking with purpose!

Fashioned and created from the man's side—a rib—the support, the aid.

You hold the keys to bind and to lose—Matthew 18:18 and when you get with another believer, for our purpose today, another woman! Oh yeah! It is on!

You walk in agreement; the woman walks with a mindset to do God's will and way! to assist and bring light!—the Holy Spirit is the component and the catalyst!

The compass in the woman is the Holy Spirit!

She is walking with purpose! She hosts and possesses the ability to see what men and others cannot see! She is a type and shadow of the Holy Spirit!

She renders aid; she helps, she comforts, she nurtures! What the man may not have, she brings! She is like glue! Elmer's glue (when things are not right, get a godly woman on the scene! It comes together!). The woman's ability to birth naturally and spiritually!

5. Nations—birthed from her—(Genesis 17:15–19).

When you think of nations, anyone you and I see or know is a nation. Everyone has this organization of culture, belief, actions, talk, walk, purpose, destiny, and assignment that causes many to go in the ordained direction. We are women, our Father's daughters who are chosen to help push them forward and see steps with more clarity given by the Holy Spirit. The faith we have given by our Daddy helps us to be, believe it, receive it, and conceive it! Yes, believe it until you see it come to pass. Sometimes, labor pains are just what they are labor pains. The work, sweat, and tears are worth it. What we have to birth out is not ordinary! Say this out loud; I am not ordinary! Scream it out loud if you have to! *I am not ordinary! I am supernaturally extraordinary! Hallelujah!* I know that it felt good to say it. Sarah laughed at the assignment, but that did not stop her from giving birth to the promise that was spoken by God. Let us receive the promise and birth it out while laughing at the same time. This time our laughter is rejoicing because we have been given the command to rejoice, and again, I say rejoice.

While we are rejoicing, God is rejoicing also over us with His song, according to Zephaniah 3:17 (MSG), it is delightful. Yes, we are doubly blessed with a song to birth.

So, as we think of Sarah, just considering how she was changed from one stage to another. Sarah received a name change—no longer was she just Sarai, she was Sarah!—a mother—one who can give birth and laugh knowing that her Father loves her and gives her great gifts, and He fulfills promises!

> And God said to Abraham, as for Sarai your wife, you shall not call her name Sarai; but Sarah [Princess] her name shall be. And I will bless her and give you a son also by her. Yes, I will bless her, and she shall be a mother of nations; kings of peoples shall come from her. Then Abraham fell on his face and laughed and said in his heart, shall a child be born to a man who is a hundred years old? And shall Sarah, who is ninety years old, bear a son? And [he] said to God, oh, that Ishmael might live before You! But God said, Sarah your wife shall

bear you a son indeed, and you shall call his name Isaac [laughter]; and I will establish My covenant or solemn pledge with him for an everlasting covenant and with his posterity after him.

Genesis 17:15–19 (AMP)

A kingdom woman, she is nation driven, mother of nations—the people in your neighborhood, at your job, in your church, anyone you encounter is a nation!

Inside of them is a nation! The more you touch someone, the more nations are changed and affected!

Sarah: Mother of Nations

Esther: Warrior of Nations

Eve: Life-Giver of Nations

Mary: Generated worship at the declaration of who she was—Blessed and highly favored.

Phoebe: Woman of Nations—Delivering the word—Romans 16:1–2.

Debra: Judge of Nations

Rachel: Keeper of Nations

Tell yourself—"They did not know that I really am a jewel!"

They did not know you were chosen; you were favored, preferred, called out; they did not know your purpose, your destiny!

So, here you are with a purpose! A woman called to worship, all these gifts and ministries on the inside of you! Hosting the Father!

They did not realize you were a diamond in the rough, Full of Love—Passion— Power—Influence—Joy—Living waters!

They just did not know!

You were fashioned—fabric! Yes, you are!

Unusual, unique colors, designs, textures, woven, knitted, made.

Be the woman who walks with purpose! Maintained by the Holy Spirit and full of His love! You are a woman walking with purpose!

Worshipper, Oracle, Multifaceted, Empowered and anointed, nations birth from you! Yes, you.

The word "women" has five letters—meaning the number of grace and favor, and our scripture came from Peter—which means rock!—Not easily moved!

He was the one who allowed the revelation to come when he said, "Thou art the Christ" (Matthew 16:16, NKJV).

Women, you are a revelation! Walk in it!

Holy Spirit, I bless you for revealing who we are as women walking with purpose! May you be the one who continues to guide us and give us the *open* heaven revelation and give us what is on the Father's heart! In Jesus, the Christ name! Amen!

"Extraordinary"

These words spoken paint a picture and develop a true image of who we are. The Word of God says that we are blessed, and we are to show that everywhere we go.

I am extraordinary, happy, spiritually prosperous, beautiful, wonderful, unique, set apart, called, chosen, designed, fearfully and wonderfully made, unusual, strange, excellent, deserving attention, peculiar, royal priesthood, major, defined, established, sweet, loving, kingly, queenly, anointed, appointed, purposed, destiny, holy, righteous creative, gifted, talented, lovely, overflowing, teeming with ideas, all woman! Astonishing, worshipping, exuberant, amazing, odd, surprising, particular, exceptional, remarkable, great, high energy supernatural, not of this world, ambassador, terrific, sanctified, purified, consecrated, connected, developed, dedicated, valued, treasured, confident, truth seeker, designed, wealthy, healthy, wise, sensitive, happy, joyous, strong, capable, defined for greatness, solid, qualified, synchronized, aligned, focused, covered, loved, marvelous, virtuous, innovative, witty, courageous, brave, dynamic, conscientious, totally awesome, splendor, walking in covenant, seeker of God's heart, God chaser, developing in the anointing, surrounded by His glory, full of his love, graced, blessed, highly favored, protected, shielded, just cool like that, smart, intelligent, wearing the best, going first class in life, full, incredible, watchman, intercessor, warrior, worshipper.

You say, extraordinary, faithful, generous, giving, redeemed, radical, on fire for Jesus, kind, self-controlled, patient, loyal, joyous, unrecognizable, healed, set free, released, kingdom girl, Holy Ghost girl, Jesus girl, Christ girl, walking in the enlarged place, outstanding, soaring like an eagle, satiated with wonderful things, lines in pleasant places, drinking of sweet and unusual rivers of living waters, exuding his sweet fragrance of worship, dripping and saturated with a new oil, drinking of the new wine, freedom girl, glowing and burning for Jesus, blazing with his glory, illuminated with his light, submerged in his spirit, new treasures and mysteries released, did I mention, victorious, triumphant, champion, supernaturally charged, full of dreams, overflowing with vision, eyes enlightened, extraordinary woman, you are awakened to beauty, truth, power, holiness, purity, walking with beautiful feet, carrying the Gospel, treasure hunter clothed, with strength, redeemed without money by God.

Hallelujah! Hallelujah!

Peace publisher, nation builder! Kingmaker!

Extraordinary woman.

Break forth in a new song!

Extraordinary woman. Turn your eyes to the Author and Finisher of your faith!

His eyes are turned toward you!

Your fabric is not like anyone else.

Extraordinary

You are intertwined and woven with many different colors, hues, hints, and tints.   Even though you may have been bruised, boxed in, and maybe even had a few dents.

Extraordinary woman, you are a kingdom builder.

Soul prospering with the thoughts of God!

Valued, kept. May I say, well kept, peace multiplied, wealth multiplied, radiant, gates opened continually to receive the wealth of the nations, walking in the unforced rhythms of grace, strategic, gracefully enhanced, favored like Esther, industrious like Lydia, innovative and smart like Phoebe, wise like Hannah, blessed and covered like Ruth, laden with gold like Queen Sheba, discerner like Deborah, courageous like Jael, prophetic like Anna.

Yes, extraordinary!

Calculated by God's matrix in our mother's womb cannot be figured out because God's design is not a formula; it is a masterpiece!

Arise, woman! Phenomenal woman!

You are His lady!

You are extraordinary!

No More Storm

Speaking that it is over regardless of what had manifested.

Hallelujah! Hallelujah!

You came with rain.

You blew your wind.

Did not understand the pain.

Asking and believing it would soon end.

Walking around with a bag loaded with fear.

Kept a box of tissues to catch every tear.

I worshipped, I prayed, I cried.

It seems like it kept going the harder I tried.

I turned to the left; I turned to the right.

What could I do without a friend in sight?

You see, the storm was not what was happening on the out-sides wind.

It was the doubt that tried to hide within.

But a revelation by the Holy Spirit came.

Once I called on The One True Name.

It felt like the boat was rocking, and I just held on.

The beautiful thing is, Jehovah Sabaoth, the Lord of Hosts, says you

are not alone.

While keeping my eyes on Him and my heart to be still. He says

I am Jehovah Rophe, the Lord God who heals. Stay low and be bold.

I am near and, in my arms, you, I will hold.

Stand firm, look at the rain and the wind.

Declare, decree, proclaim that it shall end.

Speak out of your mouth, change the atmosphere. Everything that was cloudy is purposed to become clear. Speaking that is over. Regardless of what showed its face, now it is time for it to be erased. Call on my name, stand true, be what I called you to do.

By faith, not by sight, by the Spirit, not by might. Open and receive the power for the things to change this very hour.

So, I say to the wind, I say to the rain. I say to the fear, I say to the pain. I say to the things that manifested out of nowhere. "Peace be still."

Just like He said, you can say to the mountain, move from here to there. By faith, peace be still.

So, I say to the debt, it is over. Money be released! Problems in marriage, it is over. Covenants of the Highest God be released! Children of disobedience, it is over. Obedience be released! Bad relationships, it is over. Healthy communications and partnerships be released! Generational curses, it is over. Generational blessings be released that have been held back. Salvations in our families be released!

I say released! They are set free now! In the name of Jesus the Christ!

Families are set free to worship the Thee!

We Declare! We decree! We prophesy! We speak of the Most High!

Release the blessings! Release the wealth! I say release the healing! Release the power! Dreams and visions released! Release the favor! I say bondages be broken; yokes be broken, release the strength, I say be free, regardless of what came, we proclaim with the one true name.

I say it is over regardless of what manifested. Peace be still! Hallelujah In Jesus the Christ name! Amen!

An Esther Moment, "It's Time to Say Something"

Well, my sister, by now, you may have realized that I enjoy the Book of Esther. The story of her life has so much for us to learn from, and we have such a rich treasure to draw from how she walked through the paths to get to her King.

Here we go. Esther 4:14 states,

> For if altogether silent this time, relief and deliverance themselves will stand up for the Jews from another place. But as for you and your father's house, your people will perish. And who is there knowing whether it is for a time like this that you have attained to royal dignity?

Esther 4:14 (New World Translation)

Background according to me: A beauty pageant is held, and Esther, a poor young orphan (I call it a girl from the hood), was announced queen due to the favor of God and was pleasing to the King. She was given beauty treatments—taught how to act with the King—what to say, and all the advice she would need to be queen. Esther was favored by the Lord. Esther was a risk-taker. She is alone in the kingdom, no other family members around, no homegirls to call on the phone, no computer to send an email, no chat rooms to get advice. It is just her. She gets a message from her cousin about the planned attack on her family. She tells Mordecai, you are going to have to solve this yourself.

Her cousin/uncle/overseer quickly reminded her, "Look here, cousin, just because you are in the king's crib doesn't mean you are going to escape? That made Esther think about her situation.

Mordecai told her you were not just placed here to be cute, dress nice, wear the finest jewels, sit in the palace eating pizza and playing video games, looking at the cable, eating the best, and wearing the best clothes carrying the finest label.

Esther realizes what she is to do. She calls a fast for three days from everything and begins to believe that God shall deliver her family from destruction.

Note: Sometimes, you must move away from food and surround yourself with people who are like-minded, hearing from God. The fast was for everyone because Esther could not afford to have someone with negative thoughts around her. Everyone had to be on one accord.

Now, first, she says to herself, I cannot do this; God had placed her there for a specific purpose.

The influence we have on the situation and people in our lives is powerful when you walk in the anointing and have the favor of God in your life. You can change situations just by being there, walking into a room, speaking a word, saying a prayer. God has mighty things in store for you; you must believe you are worth it. Esther, after the fast preparation, planned and got ready for the presentation. She did not call her girlfriends. She called on the Lord.

At times, you may feel like you cannot make it, but call on the Lord; He is there. Fasting gave Esther the ability to focus on the power of her God to do what needed to be done for her enemy. She was able to recognize what her destiny was, how her influence was going to affect the next generation, and most of all, she finally understood her power.

When Jehovah has His hands on your life, people cannot mess with you and get away with it. You are covered. Though Esther was facing a difficult decision, she kept her trust in the almighty God.

There are times when I could speak or share with other young ladies and feel so honored. It is because I am quickly reminded how I will be in the presence of Jehovah's daughters. Not just any lady, but special and unique young ladies called His daughters. Daughters, who are called for such a time as this, are set in place on purpose for His perfect will. Look in the mirror; we are the women chosen to make a difference and help set someone on their destiny path.

I took a minute one day and asked the Lord God Jehovah to show me how Esther felt and what it was like for her to be in a situation that involved decision-making that would save a generation of people. The very decision she had to make would save her people. Think about it. My people. Your people.

After studying the story of Esther, I found out that we ladies of excellence must be willing to take a risk and leap out on faith. Trust God and give Him our heart to say that we believe Him and receive the victory in every area of our lives. We must be completely dependent on God. We must make an impact on others to change their lives,

We have to exhibit patience and be inspired by Jehovah God. Our confidence must rise to the faith level He has given us to speak out and against any situation that does not glorify God.

Special memo to you: In order to speak out, we must believe that we do have something to say, and we must believe that we can make that powerful impact on others.

After peering into the windows of Esther's life, we see how she was a young woman of excellence. We must develop a plan and see the roadmap of where God is trying to take us. That map is His Word.

Let us look at a puzzle that is set up. When you start to put the pieces together to form the picture, it could take an exceptionally long time to put it together without the box top with the picture on it. The Lord God has given us a road map as such in Jeremiah 29:11. He said that He knows the plans He has for us, and they are good, hope, and a future. Think about everything you need to take a trip. We can gather all the supplies and snacks, the clothes needed, and gas up the car. After doing all these things, it would not be effective unless we get the roadmap or directions to how to get to the destination.

The map of Jehovah's Word is so direct and straight. It allows us to get a clear vision and see past the woods and the fear.

Now is the time to run and burst out into the scene with wide open our eyes to see the great and mighty things I do not know. Jeremiah 33:3 outlines to us a direction that God gives us to show us ways that we never thought we could understand. He reveals the fenced-in things along the way as we travel on our journey in family, business, ministry, play, gifts, and talents. *Hallelujah*! I feel like running right now while I am writing this. He is so beautiful and great! He sees everything and knows everything, and is everywhere.

Whenever you and I come before our heavenly Father to make our requests known to Him, he wants us to come to Him like Esther. We must know that we know that He has given us the access and the authority. We cannot just run out and expect things to happen without seeing these great and mighty things Jehovah God has shown us. As we sit with the puzzle pieces of our lives, He guides us as we put each piece together.

I am so excited as I think about the ways of putting a puzzle together. Some are starting their puzzle by choosing the sections with the outlining pieces and working their way to the middle of the puzzle. Others start to find one piece and start adding the pieces from the inside out. Either way, the Holy Spirit will show you exactly the piece. Jehovah tells us all the time that He knew us before we were put in our mother's womb by Him.

The plan is already in place, and we are already destined

and designed for greatness and success. We will have a great life in God, study His Word, and make time to be with Him. We work hard with the strength that He has given us in the process. As we make our take our leap of faith and step out of the boat to walk on water, it does not always feel solid; however, when we start to walk, the water becomes this sure foundation. It's because we are not walking on the natural; we are moving on the supernatural, which is indeed Jesus. When Jesus told Peter to come out on the boat and come to Him in Matthew 14:22–33 (NKJV), it was for him to stretch his faith and go where no other man has gone before. Yes, indeed, ladies, it is our time to go and do things no other woman has done.

Our faith rises like Esther. When it strongly resonated within her what she was called to do, nothing was able to stop her.

I declare right now, as you read this, that the Holy Ghost's boldness rises in us with such a burning passion and fire that it will change everything around us to be different. Our hearts will be stirred, and our eyes will be lit up with the Holy Ghost to reach out and grab someone of the old and push them into the new! Lord God Jehovah, let it resonate and resound in us like never before. The voice of what you have called us to do in the kingdom. We will not retreat in fear; instead, we will break forth and run forward fast and strong. We break the doors down with the force of Jehovah, and we run in and grab the spoils. We break out of the place of obscurity and darkness into the place of light and freedom. We are a free generation, and we have the spirit of the living God, and He has broken the chains that had us bound.

At this very moment, take a minute to think about all the

things that Jehovah has delivered you from or what you have been freed from in your life. The power of Jehovah is greater than anything we have ever encountered, and now, we are about to take the next new steps for the next dimension of greatness. We believe that He is God, and He rewards us for diligently seeking Him in the process of walking out our freedom and getting our victory.

Esther took time to seek Him when she declared a fast in chapter 4:16 of the Book of Esther. That was her way of seeking to obtain the directions and the roadmap to take down the enemy. Wow, what a strategy. It is so powerful how Jehovah God will use a time of fasting and prayer to help break through and out of a tough situation. It is our time to seek Him and do it differently.

The power of getting into His presence is a weapon that is beyond the norm. We seek Him, and He rewards us. We seek Him; He will do the rest. Look at Habakkuk 2:3, where the Word gives us another weapon. It tells us to write the vision.

Whatever you are praying, believing, and expecting God to do, write it down. We are to keep it before our eyes and watch God work in the situation and vision. What did He say? Sistergirl, there is power in our pen. We can sit and declare with what we write.

All through the Book of Esther, declarations and decrees were written to set people free, bring restoration to a land, a name, a people, and a nation. Wow!

We have that authority! We are a chosen people, a royal priesthood! Yes, indeed, I declare right now over you as you read these words. Jehovah is not slack in His promises. That is why He said to meditate on His Word, day and night. We must get our favorite pen out and some paper and make a declaration.

We have to write it down what we believe Him to do and see it come to pass. No more sitting and wondering what is going on with the dream. Turn the television and the social media off. Make a conscious choice to get in a secret place of Jehovah God and let Him guide our pens to set nations and people free. The key promise told us in 1 Peter 2:9–10 becomes real in our life. We do not have to wonder if we are valuable or if we have significant value. We can take this promise and walk in it, live it, confess it, display it, and see it manifest in our lives. Rise woman! You are significant! You matter, and you are valuable. You are royal!

Sometimes, we must remember the commandment to make a move. It does not matter what people think or say. When you step out on faith, it is not going to feel comfortable.

I wondered what Peter was thinking when he saw all that water that Jesus was told to walk on with faith. Think about Esther sitting in her private place and praying to Jehovah about the assignment that has been entrusted to her. Yes, it seems great, but the greater One is on the scene. This is an opportunity for God to do what He said He will do through us.

Hold on to Him, make a faith step, and move into a closer walk with Him. Some years ago, I decided to take this trip to Atlanta. The trip initially started out with a few friends deciding that we were going to take a trip together; however, the trip turned out to be one that Jehovah wanted me to go on alone.

That is where my relationship with Him became this love relationship. It was one that I could sit in my hotel room and talk to Him about the most intimate things in my heart. He knew all about them; however, it was just a moment to converse with Him what was on my heart. I could cry to Him, and He would hold me. We drove around the city together. I was in a place I had never gone before, but with Him, I was not afraid. He had people in the right place to guide me and help me. They were there to watch over me and make sure I was safe on the journey to understanding me.

Wow, as I type these very words, I am so in love with Jehovah and how He is so faithful.

That is where I learned to love Him even more and trust Him to show me things and take me to new places designed just for me. Have you ever gone on a trip and realized that it was just what you needed, and you said this to yourself? "This was set up just for me." Those years ago, I was gently reminded about what He put in me from the very beginning. He showed me things, and as I studied His Word, my traveling companion, I could see the beautiful things that were in store for me during the trip. When I boarded the plane to come back to Houston, I knew I was a different person. He had changed me and transformed me in the hotel room. When I was in my cocoon in Atlanta, as I call it, He showed me how to depend on Him and declare Him as my heavenly Father, my great God. Even to this day, He holds me close whenever I am assigned great tasks.

Any time I am about to make big decisions or be refreshed in the anointing He has for my life, I can talk to Him. He listens. He cares. He knows. Yes, He knows. That is so beautiful and awesome.

Let Us Pray Right Now

Heavenly Father, thank you for choosing us as Your girls. We are Your daughters enriched in every way. You have made us wealthy because of You. Anytime we have felt fear, You have removed it and replaced it with faith. Thank you for showing us that You are there, and You will never leave nor forsake us. We are so thankful for You saving us and keeping us. We appreciate You and worship You for who You are and how You guide us daily.

Thank you for opening the treasures of heaven and letting us know we are Your special treasure. We honor You and bless You for hiding us in Your wings and keeping us safe even when we were scared to take those steps into the new place. Thank you for the Blood of Jesus that protects and speaks on our behalf. Holy Spirit guide us and let us hear what is on the Father's heart that we are walking with the unforced rhythms of grace, and we are in tune with what the Father is saying for us His girls. We declare today that we are our Father's daughters.

We decree we walk in our God-given authority, and we exercise the dominion that You have given us. We bless You and honor You. We ask for forgiveness and repent for every time we have walked in places of low self-esteem and unhealthy relationships where we sought to get value through the things.

We know that we are valuable to You, and that is what we believe and accept in our lives now. We have everything we need in You, and that You alone will guide us to the things and people that will fit in the puzzle pieces of our life. Thank you for making us fearfully and wonderfully made. Hallelujah! We are strong in You, and we are favored in You. Glory to Your name! May Your presence surround us as our strong shield as we walk as our Father's daughters! In Jesus, the Christ name. Amen!

Now, do you not feel better? I do. Sometimes, it is imperative for us to stop and drop to our knees and talk to our Daddy. It is so sweet and lovely to commune with Him at any given time.

"Getting Dressed in The Holy Ghost"

Esther had the favor of God in her life. She can go to the King and get what she wants—Her enemies were trying to take her out, but God gave her a plan, a strategy on how to turn the enemy's traps he set for her back on himself. Despite the obstacles she faced, Esther was equipped to do whatever the Lord had assigned and required for her to do. Yes, we are equipped, graced, called, chosen, favored, and qualified with the anointing He has placed on our lives. In the Book of Luke 4:18–19, Jesus Christ of Nazareth stood up, grabbed the Book of Life, and boldly declared who He was, why He was sent, and what He was going to do. Yes, indeed, we have the power to grab hold of the Book of Life, Jehovah's Word, boldly declare who we are, why we are sent, and what we are going to do. That is a shout and praise right there. Hallelujah! We are anointed and appointed by Jehovah!

Esther was spiritually prepared, specially prepared for this time, and she was called as a young person to do the will of the Father. Regardless of your age, it does not mean that you are not capable of doing the Lord's will. Paul instructs Timothy in 1 Tim 4:12–16 to take heed to himself and the doctrine regardless of his age. We have to be an example in word, in conduct, in love, in spirit, in faith, and in purity. I love it. The Word of God is so pure that it is not tainted. Our purity is especially important. Let me share with your purity matters in everything. Jesus made it a point to tell the multitudes as He gave a sermon on a mountain with the disciples around him.

He outlined The Beatitudes, known as declarations of being blessed.

Jesus starts off with the spirit of a person and then continues to show that the purity in our heart is blessed, and we can see God, according to Matthew 5:8. Our hearts, the core being of who we are, are required to be full of pure, untainted, clear, undefiled thoughts, motives, actions, deeds, words, and love. Most of all, love. We are created in His image, and in His image, we love with a pure heart. We are our Father's daughters.

We are unique, different, and special in our way. God did not make copies; we are original. We do not try to compete or try to be like someone else because we have so many special qualities. He, Jehovah, is waiting on us to say, "Okay, Father, have Your way in me. Work in me to do Your goodwill and good pleasure for Your glory." No one can smile like you; no one can create like you; no one can do what you do. Accept, no, wait a minute, *boldly accept it now*. Accept the fact and know that you are set apart and called by God.

Say it unapologetically, say it with no fear, say it, and believe it in your spirit. Let the Holy Ghost rise in you and let *Him have His way!* You will be excited, enthused, and infused with an extravagant grace to break through the walls and barriers that were set up by the enemy. Say this with me, "The walls are down now in Jesus the Christ name!" Amen!

We are ladies of excellence. We are ladies of elegance. We use what we have, and that is the anointing, the gifts, and ministries of the Holy Ghost to accomplish the greater that Jesus promised in John 14:12–14 with a quickness. We do not hide behind the makeup; we put aside the clothes and outfits that are calling the wrong attention.

When you get dressed in the morning, imagine Jesus is sitting next to you, and He is helping you choose your outfit. What do you think He would say if the jewels were showing through the blouse and the skirt was too high? What about the personable under the clothes?

That is why they call them underwear. They should not be seen. They should be private. Yes, I know, you may be saying these are my clothes, but you are called to be a lady of excellence. This level of excellence has a different dress attire. Let the beauty that is within that Jehovah has placed be seen first, then the outfit.

That is what it is, the outer fit. The inner will shine so bright that the outer fit will compliment who you are and bring a sweet enhancement. A whole you is the complete real you. Let the natural beauty that God has given reflect the beauty of Him. Cultivate inner beauty and watch the outer beauty gush forth. When we allow Jehovah to work on our hearts, His excellence begins to flow out like a healing balm. You will want to dress like the royalty you are because being the King's daughter has a certain wardrobe. In other words, dress how you want to be addressed. Have you seen a king's daughter? What does she look like? How does she talk? What can you sense about her dignity, elegance, beauty, and her presence? How does she respond when addressed or greeted? Such elegance and grace attributes are our portions as our Father's daughter.

We are set apart from other ladies. Remember, in 1 Peter 2:4–10, we are chosen to be accepted and named among royalty. Wow, what a privilege and honor to be named among the kings, priests of Jehovah's kingdom. It is not just given to anyone; you have to be chosen and accepted into the beloved. Yes, Lord, we accept our royalty status and stop acting like the world's kings. There is no comparison and no competition. We are called to be different, live differently, and function differently.

There was a time when I did not realize how important that was, but when the Holy Ghost started to minister to my heart, I started seeing all kinds of things change in my life. The people around me and my surroundings started changing without me working hard to do it.

All because I decided to stand up and receive my royal status, heavenly Father handled it for me. Esther, in 2:7–10, was brought into a place where she went through months of beauty treatments before she was presented to the king. During that time, she was being prepared for her unveiling and revealing. Take time to study yourself, stand in front of the mirror, and look at what God wants to do in you. He wants to redress you, teach you how to walk like royalty, changing your speech from doubt to faith.

I just think about Proverb 20:15, you can have all the jewels, rubies, and precious stones, but the most precious of all stones are the lips of knowledge. Jehovah tells us that these are precious jewels. Lord God Jehovah, may our lips be of knowledge and precious jewels.

Beautiful things can flow from our lips when we allow Jehovah to teach us what to say at any given time. Because we have lips of that pure heart and graceful lips, the king will be our friend and will we have favor, according to Proverb 22:11. He wants to show how to flow from being a princess to a queen. We are royalty. We are our Father's daughter.

Even though she was a poor orphan, God had a specific plan for her; it did not stop her from being the best she could be. She made an impact. She understood her power. She recognized that she could be an influence. She realized that her body was precious and not a tool. She owned her presence. Hear me, woman. Own your presence. Do not let anyone else own your presence, where they can push you to do things or say things that are out of character for a woman of royalty. The image that God has created is not anyone else's. It is God's image; remember that. It is important and a strong note to keep in mind that hearing kingdom gossip is only for you to pray and allow God to reign over it, in it, and about it. Be royal. Be kingdom. Be true. Be excellent. Be.

Esther kept to herself and studied what needed to be done to win the King's favor and his heart.

There are three components that are necessary to be taken care of for us to be the ladies of excellence we need to walk in daily.

Spirit—We cannot afford to let our spirit man be defiled or junked up with all kinds of drama and negative emotions. We need to protect our spirit from bad music, wrong television shows, unhealthy books, friends, and magazines, and most of all, conversations that would cause our spirit to be polluted. We must take ownership of what we participate in and allow to come into our surroundings.

Be careful with what you let come in to take up residence in your space. If you eat junk, your bodies resemble junk and what comes of you reflects what you have eaten. Eat healthy food; then, you can experience a strong, healthy lifestyle. Ladies of excellence do not go to every movie that flashes the screen and listen to every song that comes across the radio dial. Our friendships are important, again, so important that we are commanded to watch the company we keep. The Word of God tells us to know that if the company someone keeps is corrupt, it will change the morals of that person. Do a friendship evaluation. Does this friend treat you with respect, can they pray for you, or can they get the Bible and find the scripture for you in your situation? Better yet, can they send a request for intercession on your behalf? What is important to your spirit, man, keep God turned on all the time.

I want to share a story with you. When I was thinking about this time in my life and how I was my relationship with a young man was so out of tune. The name is left out to protect the innocent. He was not exactly a Christian; well, he was not a practicing believer at the time we were forming a relationship. He wanted to watch movies, go to the dance clubs, but I could not and would not be due to my commitment to God. Eventually, we had to sever the ties because we were not equally yoked for what God had ordained for my life. What he wanted to do totally violated my morals and goals to be a pleasing vessel unto our heavenly Father.

Fill your spirit with the Word of God. Feed on It. Eat it. Drink It. Breathe It. Live It. Seek the power of the Holy Spirit. Let Him show you how to get to the Lord through prayer and fasting.

The power scripture, 2 Timothy 3:15–17, informs us of how to take the Word of God and let it teach us about what is real and wrong in our lives. God wants us to prosper as our soul prospers. This means that God has a plan for us to walk in total healing inside and out. An important note for us as women who follow our heavenly Daddy's plan is to listen and follow through with 1 Peter 2:11, which lets us know that we should avoid doing things that would cause our bodies to fight against our spirits. In other words, we should look for things and have actions that will work with our spirit, not against it. If it does not line up with the Word of God and your spirit man, then do not partake in it.

Okay, here is another story for you. This time in my life was important to me because it is when I realized more than ever that I needed a Savior, and I needed Him to be real in my life. I did not just want to be a person who mentioned Jesus but had a relationship with Him. A real relationship with Him is what was going to bring me out of all the darkness of the wrong and unhealthy relationships, to fill me with an over-flowing, powerful, deep, rich love that would never fade. I was dating this young man in college and was still very naïve about a lot of things.

I was this young girl, without a natural father living, and was still learning a lot about the men that came around me. I was still trying to find that love that I later realized was coming from my heavenly Father.

This certain day, he asked me to meet him at his friend's house. It was late in the evening, but I said *okay*. Now, my spirit was telling do not go, but my flesh was saying go ahead and go; what could it hurt? Well, I got to his friend's home. First, I should have known that this was not going to be a good experience, by the friend's name. Anyway, there were all kinds of evil and weird stuff sitting around in his apartment. I sat down and noticed he was cutting up steak. I asked him if he was about to cook, and he promptly replied that he was about to feed his dogs. These big dogs were in a room by themselves. He said that is their room. Okay, I was sitting in an apartment with someone I did not know, who obviously had a totally different lifestyle than I had. So, immediately, I started a conversation about the Lord to get an idea about his thoughts and ideas. You guessed it. He was not into the "God stuff and did not believe in God." Some may say you should have talked to him more, but at that time, I realized it was time for me to make the first step towards the door and go to my car. So, I politely told him that I would wait for my friend in my car and proceeded to get to my car with a quickness. All along the walk, yet running to my car, I just prayed and thanked Jesus for getting me out of there.

Trust me; it is best to listen to your first thought, which is the Holy Spirit. He is always looking out for us. Yes, He is.

The Word tells us that we are different, and we cannot

go to all kinds of places and be around all types of people. We just must be comfortable and accept that we are called to be set apart from the world's ways standards. I can guarantee you that if my daddy were living, I would not have pushed the envelope and made that trip to the apartment. Our heavenly Father has so much for us girls, and He loves us so much. We are His treasures, and we must see ourselves as such. Be separate and set apart may not feel good all the time, but if we do it with joy, it will please Him, according to 1 Peter 2:19–20. We should make it our aim to have a gentle and quiet spirit with 1 Peter 3:3–4 as the inscribed in our hearts. It helps us to understand that beauty comes from the inside, not the outside.

Let Us Pray

Heavenly Father, thank you so much for everything You have put inside of us. May we walk with the outstanding beauty You have placed within us. Allow it to be used for Your glory and Your purpose in our lives. We ask forgiveness for walking around and being involved in things or connected with people who tried to taint or pollute our spirits. May our hearts be pure and focused on the perfect will You have designed for us. May our hearts be filled with Your presence and strong love. We know You love us, and we give You our love. Show us more of Your ways and thank you for the Blood of Jesus applied upon our lives and thank you for the wisdom of the Holy Spirit. I believe You when You say that You know the plans You have for us, and we now walk with that plan. We honor and worship You. Thank you for Jesus, the Christ who is now at Your right-hand making intercessions for us. We now walk in our authority and truth. Hallelujah! In Jesus, the Christ name. Amen.

Body—It is particularly important to pay attention to it to do God's will, according to 1 Thessalonians 4:4–5.

A lady of excellence protects her body. We are given a sweet message that God is for our body in 1 Corinthians 6:13–20. We do not pollute our bodies with sex, sin, overeating, under sleeping, mistreating it, or letting someone else mistreat it in any kind of way.

Keep it precious as it is a treasure. Be holy as the Lord God Almighty is holy; 2 Corinthians 5:14–18 basically tells us that we are not just to hook up with anyone and think it is okay. Look at I Corinthians 6:12–20, "Your body is not yours; you just can't do what you want to do with it. You are taking Jesus with you everywhere you go, and He is watching everything you are doing. If you are not married, you should be concerned with the affairs of the Lord." In other words, you should be doing God's work, as it shows us in 1 Corinthians 7:32–35.

Let us talk about an especially important subject that many have caused a lot of controversies. Yet, there should be no controversy at all. Jehovah God created one man and one woman in the beginning with a certain purpose in mind for marriage and relationships. His will is for man and woman to be together. Pick up your Bible and read Genesis 2:15–25. Clearly, it must be stated and enforced that homosexuality and lesbianism are not of Jehovah God. If you have been in that world, know that there is freedom for you today. Decide right not to repent and turn away from it. Accept what Jesus has done for you on the cross and receive Him as your personal Lord and Savior. Invite the Holy Spirit in to fill you and guide you in your life as a believer of the Highest God. All the unhealthy conversations and laws that have allowed people to say that they were born that way and want to be free are not of Jehovah God.

He has an order, and that is man and woman in the proper statutes of marriage.

In Esther, chapter 2, when she first arrives on the scene, she immediately found favor by the caregiver of the harem of girls. He placed Esther in the best part of the palace, gave her the best of foods, he was looking out for her with special care. He gave her several attending maids. When it was time for Esther to be presented to the King, everyone admired her beauty, including the King. She was fitted for her status. So, ladies of excellence, it is important for us to get exercise, get rest, eat right, and meditate on God's Word for our physical being. Hit the track, drink water, listen to classical music occasionally.

Enhance your knowledge and mind. Get discipline now with your spiritual life, such as study God's Word, get your heart right. God has a need of you in every way. He wants to unlock the door to all the potential inside of you. It is time to show the world the whole new you. You were created with the purest quality of life in you. God has chosen you for His highest purpose.

Let us look at 2 Timothy 2:20–26. If you stay away from the drama, God can use you. You are like the expensive dishes made of the purest gold, not wood and clay, for the kitchen. Which would you want to eat an awesome meal prepared on, fine china or a wood plate? You are special; wouldn't you like to be used by God in a precious way?

He has a specific plan created especially for you. Nobody else can do it. You are the only one who can complete it. If you do it, He will find someone else. How about we choose to do those beautiful, awesome, amazing things? He is waiting.

The Mind—"He did not give us a spirit of fear, but of power, love, and a sound mind" (2 Timothy 1:7–8, NIV). It is now time to elevate our minds, ladies of excellence. Use it the way God intended you to use it. The Word of God is a promise to us that we are powerful, and we can do whatever He has set for us to do. By receiving the Holy Spirit, you will not be afraid to tell others about God and His mighty works through His Son, Jesus the Christ. It is important to renew your mind daily, according to Romans 12:2, and keep your mind steadfast on Him, just like it tells us in Isaiah 26:3.

It is a must to decide which music will feed your spirit and keep you focused on God's plan for your life. You cannot straddle the fence. You are going to the left or the right. Choose you this day whom you will serve. Make a choice to live for God and serve Him, and Him only. Choose life or death as Joshua told them in Joshua 24:14–16. I beseech you, my sisters, choose life, choose God.

Choose the good life, the things that only He can do and only He can show you. You will not regret it. Let us follow Philippians 4:8 when it gives us another lady of excellence statute to walk by daily. We are to choose to think one thing that is true, noble, just, pure, lovely, good report, virtuous, and praiseworthy.

When you have found favor with God, your enemy's traps that were set for you will be rendered null and void. In the book of Esther, Haman's trap is turned on him. God has His hand on your life. Know that in the fullness of your heart. You prepare to do your job by putting on your best outfit. It is time to meet the King. Just think, God knows who you will be with, and when it is time to meet him, he will not be able to deny the inner beauty that has been cultivated by the Holy Spirit and the Lord Himself. Let Jesus tend to the garden of your heart. He is removing all the old rusty boards, and now he will give you beautiful landscaping that will reflect a true gardener's work. Be careful to follow the godly advice you receive along the way. It can be from your parents, your pastors, spiritual leaders. Most of all, take time to listen to the Holy Spirit. Learn to hear God's voice and feel the rhythm of His heartbeat. Be sure to develop discipline. This discipline is not just about the food and physical; moreover, it is about the spirit. Practice spending time alone with the Lord so that you will know yourself and what He has in store for you. Know your own fragrance and how it is to be released to fill the atmosphere you are around. The more you allow Him to work, the more His fragrance will exude from you. He will honor you in many ways that will be a blessing to others.

Lady of excellence, here are a few other tips that will cause you to function well in the palace because you are your Father's daughter, and you are preparing to be a queen for your king.

Watch your speech—1 Peter 3:10 and Ecclesiastes 10:12. Let your words reflect God's purity and love. Do not talk too much, take time to listen first, be peaceful. Our speech should be gracious, as it states in Matthew 15:18. Most of all, let Him supply you with what to say. You can find this special tip in 1 Peter 4:11. Remember, pleasant words are like a honeycomb sweetness to the soul and health to the bones (Proverb 16:24). Righteous lips are the delight of kings, and they love him who speaks what is right (Proverb 16:13). You are precious to God (1 Peter 2:9-10). Sanctify yourself, take off the old, and put on the new. Discard the junk that has tried to clutter your heart that would try to flow out of your mouth. Develop character, integrity, and purge the old ways.

Here is something that I have shared in one of my other books. I share that it is always time to take a spiritual bubble bath with the Lord.

Bathe in His Presence with this special *soap*. We bathe every day naturally, so it is time to saturate ourselves with the soaking of His love and care. He tends to us in every way, and when He does, He wipes away the hurts, the fears, the pain, the rejections, the ridicule, and everything that came along with those heavy emotions that try to rise just when you are taking your strong steps of purpose and destiny. As the inside is getting right, He is taking care of the outer you. So beautiful.

Surrender to His perfect will—why settle for second best when He will give you His best.

Obedience—Be willing and obedient; you can partake of the good of the land. He alone will change the bitter waters to sweet for you.

Accept—Go ahead and agree with the amazing and extraordinary plan that Jehovah God has for you. He chose you, and you did not have to stand amongst a bunch of other girls to wait. He chose you first. Yes! Agree! Receive! Believe! Run! Go! Do it! You are more than able to conquer the land!

Pray—Ask the heavenly Father for guidance and direction. He is the loving Father that sits and watches while His little girl dresses for the junior dance, the senior prom, her wedding dress, her dance with the date, and approves of the man who loves her, preaching, teaching, serving, giving, loving, crying, laughing, and deciding. You name it; heavenly Father wants to be there right in the middle of it all. Ask Him; He has the answers with love.

Take some time to meditate on God's goodness—prepare to be used by Him. Cancel out fear. When it comes to saving your family and yourself, you must step out on faith and believe that God is for you and trust the Word He said to you. Now, you can make the move.

When you have purified yourself before God, you can come to the throne room and talk to Him. He will give you the treasures and tell you things that you do not know. It will be wonderful. Purity in our lives allows us to hear God more clearly. We get to heights that no one else can think about going. Opportunities come, and God shows up so we can glorify Him in all kinds of ways.

He will do that in our prayer time, work, play, quiet, relaxation, and worship. Remember God has a plan for you. Don't you want to see it? He is wonderful, and He has many loving ways to display it to us. Let Him in today. Give Him a chance to keep you in His will.

Allow Him access into your heart to love on you. He will never let you down. It is now time to grow in Christ, live blessed and be the victorious woman because you are your Father's daughter.

Take a minute to pray and declare that you are chosen for such a time as this (Esther 4:13–14). You are purposely chosen. Hallelujah! You are blessed and highly favored (Luke 1:28).

"It Is Just Our Beautiful Voluptuous Grace"

Here I am, sitting and thinking of all the things I have done or tried to do to make my standards appropriately match others to conform. Those times of downplaying the gifts and the abilities to accompany the plans of others, not realizing it was causing me to stifle the wells that Jehovah had originally ordained to flow in me. As a young girl growing up, I would encounter much ridicule, rejection, harsh words, disassociation, and verbal abuse from others who seemed to have a much cuter face or finer body, so I thought.

As we make choices for friends and relationships, we first carefully consider the wisdom of the Holy Spirit as He guides us in our selections. The beautiful part of all this, my parents all made sure that we received what we needed to get past the stereotypes and issues that many encounters. As an authentic, beautiful woman of grace, Jehovah has allowed me to break through those places and to see where and who I called me to be. You may now be asking what our beautiful, voluptuous grace is.

It is our place of being heavily loaded and filled abundantly with the gifts, talents, resources, grace, beauty, love, outstanding attributes, brilliance, worship, giving, patience, generosity, help, and we can have several attributes.

I am a woman with curves, and for years, I tried to get rid of those curves with diets, foods and distancing myself from others because I was afraid they would not agree with who I was or understand the value and worth I bring to the table. The truth is that our heavenly Father gave us our value when He created us and said that we are His. Wow, what a revelation. I am His, and that alone is priceless. So, when I came to the realization that we have more to offer than just the outside characteristics, it changed my whole perspective about my weight. My curves are voluptuous, they are there, and I will not let them be used as a hard, but will turn it into a blessing. As I exercise and watch how I eat, I am doing it because I love Jehovah, and I love me. It is a difference. It helps me to understand how to flow and make it happen.

I came across a certain translation of the scripture in Ephesians 3:17–20; this word of God gave me the power to break out of the shell that held me in for years. This scripture tells us that we have the dimensions of our Father's love. It is the fullness (the curvy and voluptuous) and grace. The ability to do it better and with more than enough given to us to accomplish so much more. Wow, it is our voluptuous grace. We have His depth, breadth, length, and height of His all-abounding love. Then He says that we are rooted and firmly placed in His love with sure confidence. No one can take that away from us. We can take our different shapes, sizes, and hearts to do the will of His heart. Purpose is calling out and saying, "Stand up and stand out." Be who I called you to be. He knew he would have all types of body shapes, but that does not stop Him from loving us. He loves you and I all the more. Yes indeed. The Word of God says that He is mindful of us and that He will bless us.

When we think of all the things that we need to receive our breakthrough, that strong light starts to shine, and the compass on the inside starts to pull us in the right direction. Our heavenly Father has already put in us what we need. We are the jewels that have been hidden for so long, and some of us have been caught up in many things and hanging around the wrong people. Our environment helps shape us, and the words from our mouths are like our guide. When we speak what the Lord God has said in His Word, we will start to see exactly what He wants to see. Greatness is our portion, and we must know that so we can flow.

Every time you reach that place of wonder, stop and remember where your steps should be taking you. If you see hard places, then stop and remember that God said that he had made that rough place smooth. All the issues and matters of the heart are generally a misstep in the Word. Somewhere, somehow, we as women have traveled into a place that was not healthy. We, then, make a choice to go after the wholeness and promises of God. Take a few minutes and ask the Holy Spirit to show you where you need to clear out the cobwebs and grab hold of your voluptuous grace. The fullness, overflow, beauty, redemption, and resurrection power of Jesus the Christ are already working. It never stops. It reminds me of when our heavenly Father put a rainbow in the sky. In Genesis 9:9–13, He made a promise that He would put a rainbow as a sign in the sky to represent His covenant promise. He set it there, and it has not moved. There are times when we are going through our moments of doubt and disbelief. Then we halt all the negative words, thoughts, actions and cancel every fear that is feeding into the unhealthy diet. We must remember the promise that He made and look for the rainbow in every situation. The rainbow naturally appears when it has rained. Generally, scientists and the weather subject matter experts would say that the sun is shining through the rain. Wow, did you hear me? I will say that again. The rainbow appears when the sun is shining through the rain at the time the water droplets are falling, I am amazed at this. So, let us have a review, ladies. You mean to tell me that when I am going through and have my eyes filled with tears is when I should stop and allow the Son to come in the middle of it. This is powerful. The Son, Jesus the Christ is right there to give us some tissues (I call it joy paper) to wipe our eyes and look for the promise of Jehovah's Word for our situation. Then we can immediately see the rainbow in the sky. There are times when there is no rain in the sky, but our Father will guide our heads to look up and see the beauty of His promises. Wow, He loves that much, and He will make sure we do not get lost in the drama. There are times when He will allow the rainbow to be seen in clear skies; then, sometimes, there are double rainbows. Yes, Lord! Help us, Holy Ghost, to recognize the beauty of every situation. We will exalt You! Thank you, Father! In Jesus' name! We exalt You!

We pick our heads up to see the rainbow in the sky. The angels are running around excited because we are embracing our grace and pulling on our Father's neck with a big love hug! He is right there when we go to our knees and ask for forgiveness for taking too long. His arms hold us and give us the strength to keep moving.

We are blessed, and the promises of His heart are yes and amen. At this very moment, while you are reading this and I am writing this, we throw our hands up, receive his love and mercy, stand up in our voluptuous grace and do the kingdom assignments He has assigned to us like we've never done it before! We are bold, brave, beautiful, courageous, strong, wise, graceful, authentic women. Yes, my sister, we are our Father's daughter. We are equipped, chosen, and anointed to do everything that is set for us to do. He loves with an everlasting love, and that is the truth.

I always share this message with every lady I meet that we should know for ourselves that what He has designed is a masterpiece. We are fearfully and wonderfully made. Every lady has something different about her that is so sweet and unique. If you try to copy or be in direct competition with other women, you then take away from yourself. He lets us know that we have been crafted and skillfully wrought in such a way that it becomes a priceless piece of art. When we go to art stores and look for that special piece of wall art, we have a certain eye for color and lines. We reach out to touch to see if it is authentic. You know the realness of the masterpiece. Yes, our heavenly Father has created us with an outstanding special seal that cannot be matched.

When you look in the dictionary and any other book referencing words and their meanings regarding authenticity, you should see your picture. I see my picture when I look up the definition of authentic and every reference about it. Our individual assignments are powerful, yet we are called to connect with others. Our masterpiecefulness, I just create that word. Yes, I can create a word because the Creator is in me. Masterpiecefulness describes the ability and the capability to hold the unique design and craftsmanship of the Artist. This Artist is Jehovah. He has put His stamp of approval on us. He has signed it with His name and covered us with the Blood of Jesus. Then, on top of that, he uses a special oil in the paint from the anointing of the Holy Ghost. You better give Him some praise! The power to step out of the old cardboard box and walk as a beautiful workmanship. Wait a minute, let us get it straight. We are His workmanship, according to Ephesians 2 (NLT), for we are God's masterpiece (workmanship). He has created us anew in Christ Jesus, so we can do the good things he planned for us long ago.

As we start to meditate on His promises of His Word, the rainbow becomes so clear and precise. We can see the line of the colors and how the Son, Jesus the Christ, is shining in our rain. Our RAIN is the Radiant Anointing Illuminating Now. We receive our RAIN. Every time it looks like it is the hard place, that is our place of RAIN meeting and intersecting with the Son of God. We should get excited when that takes place. This is like our Kairos moment. You may be asking what Kairos is? This is when we are experiencing a Rhema moment. Kairos moment is when it happens according to the divine timing of our God. It's when purpose and destiny connect and begin to flow together. It's the moment our heart has opened up and received the prophetic Word spoken to see it start unfolding and manifesting exactly what was spoken at the right time. The opportune time, the blessed time, the divine timing of our Father putting His super on our natural. We become the supernatural extraordinary beings we are designed to be with the extraordinary sauce. It's not us that is doing it; it's the God in us!

The Holy Spirit is releasing a special outpouring for something that you and I have been waiting for a long time. We have been praying and fasting, worshiping and praising, sowing and giving. Then suddenly, the Lord God comes in with a special grace, a special moment of unveiling a revelation or a truth that will set us free and catapult us into the next realm of our anointing. It is like He came behind us and gave us a mega push into His purpose for us. We, then, are walking in this voluptuous grace and in a new dimension of His sweet glory and favor. He saw us when we cried up and out. We cry up to Him and out of our hearts with a passion to hear Him and feel Him. He reaches out and fills us up with an overflow that has been sweetened with His love.

We start to run again because we chose to take a few minutes on "His loveseat." Our arms are strengthened, hearts renewed, minds clear, feet on fire, legs strong, back straight, and most of all, our hearts are on purpose. This is so lovely, and this is amazing because He is standing there cheering us on to keep moving when it feels heavy, keep moving when the light seems to be dim, keep moving when you are hungry and thirsty. While we are moving, He is watching every step and guiding us along the way. He promised to watch over us and order our steps as we walk in His way. Psalm 37:23 shows us as we declare it out loud, "The steps of a *good* man are ordered by the LORD, And He delights in his way. Though he falls, he shall not be utterly cast down; for the LORD upholds *him with* His hand." Yes, heavenly Father, hold our hands, we walk and take our steps on purpose with intentional strategies. We may be grown women, but we are still our Father's daughters. We may be single or married with a husband, but we are still sitting on His knee telling Him all about it. Wow, regardless of age or stature, we have the ability to call to our Daddy, and He will

guide us with the uncommon love into the uncommon places!
Hallelujah! Let's get girls! Our voluptuous grace is working!!

"A New Song in Our Mouths"

(Psalm 97:8, NKJV)

In this new place, we have a song to sing. In our new space, we are not afraid anymore because we know that our heavenly Father is with us. It is not only just a song; it is a new song. In moments of searching for answers and looking deep within, that is when we remember we have a risen King! He is there, and He knows it all, just making sure that we are standing tall. Pulling down the strongholds and keeping our hands lifted high is our song to say that our heavenly Father has caught every tear we cry. Now, these tears are turned into water that flows heart to heart. It is a new day, a brand-new start. Hallelujah!

When you take a minute to read this Psalm in many different translations, as a daughter of the Highest God, we stand and proclaim His goodness! He calls us into a secret place at that very moment to say He loves us with an everlasting love, and He is singing over us. Old melodies are good; however, when He has given us a new song. We dance to it! We shout it! We run with it and tell the whole world about it! Taking off the old clothes and wearing bring new colors.

He calls us a beautiful love song. We are His women with a lyric written in our hearts just for Him to reveal at the right time. The land of Judah means a place of praise. These ladies (the daughters of Judah) have a special inheritance, a special right to worship. Can you see them waking up with a song on their lips, working all day with a song flowing and the sound caressing the air? Yes, ladies, sisters, that is us! Open up and sing a new song! Let the air hear your voice; let the atmosphere hear your sound. Our releasing out has been held for years. The years of wondering and wandering are now a time of singing. In one of my favorite books of the Bible, The Song of Songs, it says winter has passed, and springtime has come. Well, I believe we can have springtime every day because we lift a song to Him every day. Allow the Holy Spirit to give you a new song and sing out proudly and loud! It is a new season and a new day!

Personal Ministry Time

As you take a few personal minutes, take a few minutes to hear from our heavenly Father, let him show you what he will do when we invite Him into the situation. Where you see the R put a word there that lets you know who He is, what He will do, and how It will do it. We are called for such a time as this, and we have the ability to do it without question.

E.S.T.H.E.R

*E*very *S*econd *T*hat *H*e *E*nters I am…

Radically saved, redeemed, renewed, restored, refreshed, rekindled in my love, rejuvenated, released into my purpose and destiny, renovated in my motions, reaffirmed in His love, realigned, and regenerated by the Holy Spirit, recovered, ready, represented by my heavenly Father!

Maybe you can think or find words that start with the letter "R." Ask the Holy Spirit to help you develop your own personal affirmation and confirmation of His affirming love. As you sit and reflect on His goodness and His power to set you free by the Blood of Jesus, in the name of Jesus, by the power of the Holy Spirit.

Scenario: Think about this. I have everything I need. Yes, I have seen those movies and TV shows that talk about prayer.

I have been in my prayer room, and I have a list of everything I am praying to my heavenly Father do for me. I have my Bible, tablet, books, prayer books, journal, dance garments, man, pen, paper, worship songs, blessed oil, uniform, map, so I can look at the nations, my flags, and banners to praise. I have my prayer partner in cue waiting so we can conference together to pray. Yes, it is time to go in! I am going into my secret place, and I am going to my war room (well, my closet) Either way, I am ready. Let us see. Is there anything else I need to remember to bring?

Well, this is usually how most women will decide to pray. They will grab everything that seems to be naturally right to bring into the secret place to commune with our heavenly Father. It is so funny to me because that is exactly what I would do before the Holy Spirit quickened my heart. He spoke to my spirit and immediately reminded me what was the most important to bring into the presence of our King.

He showed me that I needed an open heart, a heart of forgiveness, love, compassion, passion, truth, humility, and the desire to bow low before our heavenly Father. I needed a servant's heart that was patterned after Jesus.

I would make sure to have my knee pillow because I am going to send some knee-mail and a heart of thanksgiving to reach up and touch His heart.

So often, we are preparing for a time of prayer and assignments, but we must remember to keep our heart after God, the Giver of the assignments, and prayer time. In our arsenal, there are many weapons. An arsenal is a storage place or a collection of weapons. In my study of the arsenal, you sometimes must make sure you have a current inventory of what is in there. Some weapons are used at certain times. These weapons consist of prayer, praise, worship, works, seed sowing, fasting, quiet time, personal reflection, and a time of decrees and declarations, and *laughter*! *Yes, laughter.*

Esther used a secret weapon that we sometimes overlook. She used a tool of preparation. Her foods were carefully selected for her to eat. Her garments were chosen, as she put on her royal robe before going to the King. She chose who would pray with her, and then she selected what she was going to serve her enemy. She also had a time of preparation and pampering. It is necessary to take some time to refresh, get some proper sleep, and, as I shared previously, laugh. Oh my God!—Laugh out loud and laugh hard.

Your homework assignment is to fund a funny joke and laugh to release healing into your soul. A merry happy heart does many wonders for our bodies. Yes indeed.

It was her time in preparation to be with the King. Our heavenly Father wants to be invited into our prayer time. He wants to come in and take care of that thing or mattes of the heart that sometimes seems so heavy that they are not always easy to pray out. I had a moment of reflection and heart moments of remembering when I needed help, and I was wondering what to do as a young girl in school. It was a time for us to get out of school, it was pouring down raining, and all the children were waiting for the parents to pick them up. I was just standing there because I did not have a cell phone (it was back then, no cell phones). One of my friends said, "Come on, we can take you home." But I remembered that my mom said that my daddy would come pick me up, so wait for him. Then as I said, "No, I am waiting on my daddy," here comes the bullet silver-blue station wagon around the corner. He was grinning ear to ear. He said, "You thought Daddy wasn't coming. When Daddy tells you something, know that Daddy will be there and take care of it."

Our Daddy God is saying to us, "I said I would take care of it, and I would be here." So, our roles and responsibilities are to go to our secret place and rest. Do not fight with Him when He just wants to hold you. Let Him love on you.

So, Esther was in a situation when the enemy was going to take out her nation; she remembered what was told to her by her uncle about her heavenly Father. She strategically told the people to pray for three days and set aside that time. We must set some personal time to consecrate and believe God for some powerful breakthroughs and victories. In her time of preparation, she came with one thing that was important. It was her heart for the king. The glitter, bling, and shimmer were not her goal. It was that one thing that would help her save her nation. It was her heart for the people and all of those who were in danger.

We all have the same capacity as Esther as we seek the King's heart. When we see someone hurting, we do not turn our heads. Instead, we look for their eyes, not the shoes they are wearing or the special dresses they may be wearing. We look at their hands, despite the jewelry, and see their heart needs some powerful encouragement. This is our time to say that it is already alright. This is the time we can share with them about our King, our Daddy. Every second He enters, we are redeemed and renewed. We are given a heart of peace, love, grace, favor, strength, love, and the mighty authority to set the atmosphere with declarations and decrees. He gives us mysteries, revelations, knowledge, keys, and strategies.

Having an anointing or capacity like Esther allows us to touch another woman or person and see recognize their importance. Love begins to flow in the atmosphere and change the perspective of the matter. Let Him in and watch Him redeem you in every way possible. In Jesus, the Christ name! Amen.

"Daughters Awakened For Love at the Right Time"

"Do Not Stir up Nor Awaken Love"

(Song of Solomon 2:4–7, 8:4 NKJV)

Wow! Every time I read this scripture, it blesses me. This whole Book in the Bible is describing a love of a man for a woman and she for him. It is quite illustrative, and it gives such a strong sense of romance and love. It also depicts a symbolism of marriage and what happens once this man truly gets with the one he loves. So, throughout their conversation, there may be a few moments where it shifts to a conversation between the ladies.

She is so engulfed with her love for him and how she feels. At certain moments it is a gentle reminder from her to "Daughters of Jerusalem." I consider this to be you and I or anyone who has been or is about to enter a love relationship with a man. She describes her encounter with him at the banqueting table and how she has feasted on his delights of cakes and raisins. What is so interesting, though, is how she begins to change the words and turns to speak to the daughters and tells them not to awaken love before it is time.

I am often reminded of the scripture in Ecclesiastes 3:11: "Everything is beautiful in its time." Could it be that when we are looking for that special love, and for sure, a house, car, and other powerful events that we are trying to make something happen before its time? Yes, I think I have tapped into something here. Let us dive a little deeper. She has specifically turned to them to make sure that when it is time for this type of intimacy, one must surely be in a love-awaken state and in proper protocol. She not only tells them once, but she makes sure to tell them again.

So often, we have an idea or a thought, and we are in full speed ahead to make it happen. Even now and then, I must remind myself to say this scripture out loud so my soul can hear it. The keyword is "do not awaken love until it pleases," so, at this point, we need to be commanding love to hear our hearts and our hearts to communicate with love. We will discuss this again in more detail with the next book. Stay tuned. It will allow us to really go deeper into the things and intimacy of God.

A Special Women's
Bible Study

Gather a group of ladies and begin this study. Use it as a personal encouragement for one another and to help others develop that spiritual intimacy with our heavenly Father. Be sure to invite the Holy Ghost. He will have a lot to share. You will most definitely be blessed. We are called, chosen, and equipped. Let us use what He has invested and let the women know that we have a special place as one of His intercessors. Are you ready? We are.

Dawn Walkers and Talkers

Bless Jehovah and give reverence to Jehovah

Holy Spirit, have your way! We are standing and calling on the Most High God! He leads and guides daily. There are moments we come to Him in the early moments, and He comes to us in the early morning. We are describing a plan of intercessors chosen by God.

Read the scripture, Mark 6:45, in your favorite translation.

The Lord knows what is going on, and He is always watching. Let us think about people who daily watch and where they are sitting from their perspective to see the better view.

- ❖ The man that sits in the towers watching planes fly and land.
- ❖ The man that sits in the towers at the ports to see ships come and go. He lets the bridge up and let it down.
- ❖ You ever thought about how every time they come to work on the lights or lines, they must go up higher.

As an intercessor, you cannot just go into the lowest places when it is time to pray. There are times when you and I must go to a high place to pray.

The first thing in the morning is the time when we come to God and receive. The instructions of our day. We let the old tiredness be cast off and seek God. In this scripture, Jesus went to the mountain to pray (v.46). He went to a high place and different place—a place where everyone could not go.

The boat was in the water. He was on the land. We are praying in the midst. Jesus is watching (v.47).

He saw them struggling, and the wind was against them. At first, he was watching them all rowing and fighting against it, watching and seeing. Then it says at the first watch, which is 3 a.m.–6 a.m. The release of the manifestation of the Word of God to demolish wicked plans before the day (v.48).

It is a time to rise and shine—time to declare the Word of God over our lives.

See this section of verse in Isaiah 60:1–5 (remember your favorite translation).

Mathew 14:22–33 shows us a different way described.

It is time to come and pray.

It is time to come and seek God's love.

Hear His voice. Praying and seeking Him early in the morning.

Dawn talker and walker!

When we get up with Jesus, He is already praying.

Psalm 46:1–11—mainly (v.5)—He helps me at dawn.

God shall help me at dawn. At the break of day.

The breaking of dawn.

Isaiah 58:8—dawn fast—breaking forth like the morning—get up, fast, pray, talk to the Lord. There is significance in the early morning. The things that have crawled around in the night or tried to form at night. God Jehovah says at daybreak; I will help you.

Romans 13:11–14 (your favorite translation).

The night is far spent; it is just time to step out of the darkness. The light breaks forth in the morning. The armor of light is our clothes. Darkness is not our clothing. The power of Jehovah!

The Light Time

Arise and Shine! Our light has come! Glory to God!

❖ As Intercessors, we have to start operating in the day; nighttime is not how you are supposed to work. You can, but at some point, you will need more light.

God shows a clear example, and we can view what He did for the Israelites. It may be similar to us when the Israelites were going through. When He parted the water, the clouds looked like light to Pharaoh and light to His people. As we read and study Exodus 14:24–25, The Lord fights for us at the break of dawn. The breaking of dawn! The dawning of a new day.

Dawn talkers and walkers!

Look at Luke 1:78–80 (NKJV).

We have the Dayspring as our covenant portion. He is here! The dawn and the Dayspring are here to guide us!

As we pray, we do not have to struggle with the prayers. We just invite Jesus into the situation. The breaking of day immediately comes forth.

An intimate time between husband and wife—God and His bride—His people

Effective prayers James 5:13–17.

Psalm 57:1–11 (v.5–8).

Time to awaken the dawn, the night has been far spent, we have been dwelling on the issue of the past, the pain, the old things too long.

Think about the effective, fervent prayers of the righteous in James 5:13–17 (NKJV).

This type of prayer is one that causes the intercessor to experience a place of intense communication with our heavenly Father.

Shout with me: Awake! Awake!

Awake the dawn!

My daily awake is in Him!

The word "dawn" represents the first appearance of light in the sky before sunrise.

In other words, it is the beginning of a new day. A new time is here for us.

When we are asking for the dawn and needing the fresh new glow, we must readily turn to our heavenly Father and request His special touch with grace like no other.

Here are some points to pray when we are praying and seeking the Father during the dawn.

The Significance of the Dawn Prayer

❖ Protection

❖ Direction

❖ Instruction

❖ Solidification in the day (meaning I know God is going to do this).

❖ Confidence because He is in the boat.

    Psalm 108:1–13; focus on verse 2.

❖ The dawn represents a light before the sunrise. We pray during the fourth watch until we can see the true light!

The light! The revelation! The wisdom of what we are seeking God about.

❖ The first light of a new day or the beginning of something.

Arise of God, awaken the dawn, a new day. Take off your sleeping clothes and put on your rejoicing clothes, put on your shouting clothes. Weeping may endure for a night, but joy comes in the morning, according to Psalm 30:5 (your favorite translation).

In Jesus' name, amen!

"I Am My Father's Daughter"

Prayer Focus

This page is to write names, ideas, or anything the Holy Spirit gives you to pray and intercede on someone's behalf. As we are our Father's daughters, we have an assignment. We are about our Father's business. In Jesus, the Christ name, ask, seek, knock (Matthew 7:7, NKJV). Allow the Holy Ghost to lead and guide you in your prayers. He knows exactly what we are to pray for every time.

Brown Girl Rich Jewels

Take a few minutes to make a note of your special treasures (dreams, visions, desires, and goals). Consider what makes you special, how do you feel. What are your purposes and passions? You are unique, and you have extraordinary gifts. Time to allow yourself to *SOAR*!

Stand Out Among the Rest!

_____
_____
_____
_____
_____
_____
_____
_____
_____
_____
_____
_____
_____
_____
_____
_____
_____
_____
_____
_____
_____
_____

About the Author

Pastor Karen Denese Brown

Daughter of the Most High God.

Sharing the Gospel of Jesus and His powerful ministry, committed to the covenant of His love, blessed to be a blessing.

Pastor Karen (PK) serves in ministry at The Mountain of Faith International Ministries, under the leadership of Apostle John L. Hickman, Jr. Her global ministry includes serving the "Amplify" Women's Ministry, The Faith Girls (young women living purely on purpose class) and blesses the Lord with The Voices of Faith Praise Team.

There are no limits and no boundaries when it comes to God. "We can do all things through Christ which strengthens us." He is worthy of being praised! Most of all, she is excited about the ministry of the Holy Spirit!

Pastor Karen Brown is an international inspirational speaker, author, mentor, and coach. Her ability to reach the audience and touch their heart is uniquely designed especially for each person in attendance. PK is known for her passion for women and men to walk with the presence of God and experience His extravagantly lavished love.

Her most beautiful passion is to proclaim the Word of God to all. As an ordained pastor, she, lovingly, with sweet grace, ministers to young girls and women to walk in their awesome gift of purity and recognize their value in the kingdom. PK, purposes in her heart to make sure everyone knows who Jesus is and how to have a relationship with him. Pastor Karen has developed and established Christgirl Ministries and Publications. This ministry is developed to share with the world what young women and women of all ages can be when they have submitted their lives to Jesus Christ. We can do great works and experience great things with the power of the Most High God.

PK's most favorite fun time is hanging with her family and friends, watching old movies and cartoons, and most all, making sure she has chocolate nearby in her briefcase. Everything is always better with prayer and chocolate.

You can reach Christgirl, Pastor Karen Brown:

Email: christgirlmag@gmail.com

www.christgirlmag.org

"But seek (aim at and strive after) first of all His Kingdom and His righteousness (His way of doing and being right), and then all these things taken together will be given you besides" (Matthew 6:33, AMP).

Other Publications

> *Butterflies for God*

> *Look Again...What the World Showed You is Not How God Sees You*

> *In The Key of Love. Heart Notes Within*

Favorite Scripture

Strength! Courage! You are going to lead these people to inherit the land that I promised to give their ancestors. Give it everything you have, heart and soul. Make sure you carry out The Revelation that Moses commanded you, every bit of it. Do not get off track, either left or right, to make sure you get to where you are going. And do not for a minute let this Book of The Revelation be out of mind. Ponder and meditate on it day and night, making sure you practice everything written in it. Then you will get where you are going; then you will succeed. Haven't I commanded you? Strength! Courage! Do not be timid; don't get discouraged. God, your God, is with you every step you take.

Joshua 1:8–9 (MSG)

Endnotes

1   Wikipedia. *Purpose of wine cellars.*

2   Webster Dictionary

CPSIA information can be obtained
at www.ICGtesting.com
Printed in the USA
LVHW082354150122
708614LV00013B/394